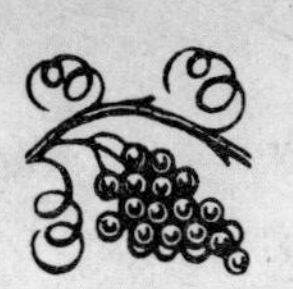

Series Editor PAMELA VANDYKE PRICE

PITMAN

Pitman Publishing Limited
39 Parker Street, London WC2B 5PB

Associated Companies
Copp Clark Ltd, Toronto
Fearon-Pitman Publishers Inc, Belmont, California
Pitman Publishing New Zealand Ltd, Wellington
Pitman Publishing Pty Ltd, Melbourne

First published in Great Britain 1979

Printed in Great Britain by
Hazell Watson & Viney Ltd, Aylesbury, Bucks

ISBN 0273 01396 3

Also in this series:
Guide to the Whiskies of Scotland *Derek Cooper*
Guide to the Wines of Bordeaux *Pamela Vandyke Price*
Guide to the Wines of Burgundy *Graham Chidgey*
Guide to the Wines of Champagne *Pamela Vandyke Price*
Guide to the Wines of Germany *Hans Siegel*
Guide to the Wines of Spain and Portugal *Jan Read*

This book is dedicated to the Rhône vignerons, négociants and officials who have made my journeys so interesting and enjoyable. My special thanks to the late Baron le Roy and his family for firing my enthusiasm, and to Pierre Ligier for twenty years patient assistance in my search for information.

Contents

Appendixes

1

The Region

The Rhône Valley will be a familiar name on route maps to the many holiday makers who journey the length of France from north to south. Unfortunately, too few people know much about this most interesting region and the wines it makes, even though they are amongst the greatest that France produces. Many wine lovers who now neglect them would certainly find Rhône wines delectable and fascinating if they took the opportunity to learn about them.

The area itself is virtually one long river valley. It shows itself on the map as an immense groove, an ancient marine ditch between the Massif Centrale on the west and the Près-Alpes in the east, and the many rock formations which tower above the river make it a fascinating place for geologists. It is curious that from one single Swiss glacier flow two of the great rivers of Europe, the Rhine and the Rhône. The Rhine flows north through Switzerland, Germany and Holland and finally reaches the North Sea; along its banks in Germany are produced some of the world's finest white wines.

The Rhône, after a short journey through Switzerland, erupts into France from the western end of the Lake of Geneva (Lac Léman) and after a 500 mile journey it enters the Mediterranean at Bouches du Rhône, near Marseille.

The Rhône is France's fastest flowing and most majestic river. It runs in all seasons, receiving water from many tributaries on its long route south, and has been described as "the furious bull descending from the Alps" (Michelet). This savage river with its tremendous volume of fast-flowing water creates enormous hydro-electric potential, so that between Lyon and the south coast there are no less than ten hydro-electric stations producing 12,000 million kilowatts every hour. On its way through this part of southern France the Rhône passes through vineyards that make some of the world's finest red wines and many excellent whites. This area—the Côtes-du-Rhône—includes six départements (provinces, each with its own préfect and each called after its principal river). These are the Rhône, the Loire, the Drôme, the Ardèche, the Vaucluse and the Gard.

As well as producing still red, white and rosé wines, there are dry sparkling wines and rich dessert wines made in this region.

Climate

The vineyards of the Côtes-du-Rhône start west of Vienne and, with certain gaps, extend southwards as far as Avignon, which is really in Provence. The region is blessed with abundant sunshine and very little rain—sometimes none for two months at a time in the summer months. In general, the climate varies between extremes: the summer, which really starts around May and lasts until September, is hot with bright blue skies and sun day after day; autumn brings thunderstorms and rainy spells, and the winter is cold and dry with temperatures low enough for snow and icy conditions—in fact the snow often remains on the top of Mont Ventoux and surrounding peaks right through the year. The rivers which flow off the slopes pour into the Rhône in torrents when the ice melts in the spring, and they continue to flow throughout the year. Thunderstorms, as with hail storms, are normally fairly localised and are a hazard to the wine grower. Very heavy storms can batter the vines and hail, particularly when the grapes are forming, can break them and spoil the crop. There is also the danger that hailstones will damage the vine itself, bruising the stems to the disadvantage of possibly more than one vintage.

In addition to these climatic variations there is the sinister wind, the Mistral, which blows directly down the Rhône Valley from the north. It has a savage, ice-cold intensity during the winter and, in an equally unpleasant way, in the warmer weather it seems to scorch and dry the vegetation and human beings—whose tempers invariably suffer at such times. Throughout the length of the Rhône Valley visitors will notice barriers of trees, including the picturesque tall dark green cypress, as well as man-made wind-breaks, which have been put up to shield the vines from the ravages of the wind, as it wreaks havoc on many crops. It bends vegetation cruelly (as admirers of Van Gogh's paintings will remember) and often simply sweeps away any loose topsoil. The vines are pruned low to help strengthen them against the Mistral: any trained high would soon be beaten to the ground.

Even the continuous summer sunshine is not, as one might think, ideal for vines: they also require adequate moisture for their food. Rainfall is irregular and tends to be heavy over short periods, the minimal periods being February and July/August, the maximal periods March to May and September to November.

The Soil

Such is the uninviting appearance of much of the soil in the rugged, varied Rhône landscape, that it might be thought that no crops could be successfully cultivated there. However, do not forget that the vine thrives where no other crop (except the olive) can be grown, and it gives of its best in many soils where it has a hard struggle to survive at all.

In general, the vineyard area of the Rhône Valley may be divided at Valence, which is the natural start of Provence, although in fact this region only really begins at Orange. North of this are the vineyards on the steep slopes of the western bank of the Rhône, except for the magnificent Hermitage vineyards at Tain. South of Valence the valley widens considerably: on the east bank is, first, the chalky plateau of Tricastin and second, further south, the alluvial plain between the Rhône and the Mont Ventoux range with terraces of rolled stones and unending vineyard vistas. On the west bank of the Rhône, the various tributaries (the rivers Gier, Cance, Doux and Eyrieux) enter the main valley through many beautiful gorges.

There are many different types of soil in the region, and even in such a small area as Châteauneuf-du-Pape there are, for example, stony soils, red soils, sandy soils and even chalky soils. The huge stones, which are one of the features of the southern Rhône vineyards, look exactly like jacket potatoes; they are so big that it is difficult to walk on them in ordinary shoes. They act rather as night storage heaters to the vines, by reflecting up on to the plants the gentle warmth which they have been storing from the strong sun during the day.

Situation

The Rhône vineyards have been famous since very early times. They are particularly fortunately situated: merchants from the Middle East could visit Marseilles by sea and also traders from the far north, coming into the Mediterranean through the "Pillars of Hercules" as the Straits of Gibraltar were called in ancient times. From Italy, routes south of the Alpes Maritimes made this part of France easy to get to, and travellers and merchants from Spain arrived along the Mediterranean shores from the west. The north-east of France, with its own crossroads leading to the north and west, was also on a natural route, and it should not be forgotten that the river Rhône itself remained a highway, both for merchandise and men, for many centuries.

It is not by chance that most of the great vineyards of the world are situated in river valleys or alongside rivers. The slopes of the banks are a naturally fertile site for vines, so the vineyards benefit not only from the moisture of the river but also from the shelter provided by the higher ground above them. It is rightly said that "A vine likes to see the river but it doesn't like to get its feet wet."

The other natural advantage of the Rhône Valley is that many varieties of vine can thrive there so that, by judicious blending, the production of a wide range of magnificent wines is ensured for vintage after vintage.

2
History of the Rhône

The whole region of the Rhône Valley and Provence shows traces of many centuries of life. Relics of the Stone Age are seen at the Neolithic cemetery at Cairanne and there are many prehistoric sites.

The earliest known inhabitants were the Ligurians, a savage tribe from Asia who lived by hunting and by the sword. They were followed by the Celts, who introduced agriculture to the region. The Phoenicians, the most astute traders of their time, also visited the area; they probably created the famous trade route from the tin mines of Cornwall across France and down the Rhône Valley to what is now the Mediterranean coast, and they also traded in amber, setting up stations along the routes they took.

Around 600 B.C. the Phoceans, Greeks from Asia Minor, began to penetrate the western Mediterranean: civilisation as we can now understand it had arrived. The Phoceans are supposed to have introduced the cultivation of the grape to Greece and Sicily and they brought it with them to Provence, where they successfully established themselves among the Ligurian-Celtic population. Their chief trading post—and the settlement that grew up around it—was Marseille (or, as it was then called, Massilia), so that this may claim to be among the oldest cities of France, if not the oldest. The Phoceans prospered, in spite of problems with the local tribes and invasions by both the Celts and various pirates who arrived from the sea. About 150 B.C. the Massilians had to appeal to the Romans to come to

Roman remains at Vaison-la-Romaine

Le Pont du Gard

their aid and save their settlements which, by this time, extended as far as what is now Nice.

Roman Influence

The Romans came, saw—and felt it worth their while to conquer. Within a generation they returned with substantial forces, not to assist the Phoceans but to add the region to their own empire.

The Roman name for the new addition was *Provincia Romana*—the Roman Province; from this came the name 'Provence'. Julius Caesar had by now conquered Gaul (France) and Roman military power brought many benefits: superb Roman roads, a greater amount of civil administration, and law and order in general. Around 42 B.C. one of Caesar's commanders founded Lyon which, in 27 B.C., became the capital of Gaul. The whole Rhône Valley was thus a great highway for important traffic. Roman culture replaced Greek and cities such as Arles, Aix, Nîmes, Orange, Vienne and Vaison-la-Romaine grew up, their forums, temples, arenas, theatres and public baths being built on a lavish scale. Aqueducts, such as the three-tiered Pont du Gard, brought plentiful supplies of water. Many of these Roman remains, magnificent even in ruin, are highly evocative of the glorious past—do not miss a chance to see any of them.

In the second half of the first century B.C. Vienne became the capital of the province and, from the time of Diocletian (about A.D. 300), it was the capital of the whole region of southern Gaul. Previously, Vienne had been important as the capital of the Allobroges of ancient Gaul, before these people were defeated by the Romans.

The Romans brought the wine vine and knowledge of its cultivation to France and, eventually, its cultivation reached as far as the Rhine. The grape followed the legions, who needed their wine ration, but it has long outlived their conquests.

These early days of viticulture were not always peaceful. In A.D. 92 all the vineyards in Gaul and throughout the Roman Empire suffered from the decree of the Emperor Diocletian that vines were to be uprooted; this was intended to increase the area devoted to the production of grain, so that granaries might be continually well stocked—the Roman public quickly made its disapproval felt if those in authority risked bread supplies running short! The wine makers of Gaul, however, had their own views about this and attributed the ban on vines to the Italian wine makers being jealous of the superior Gallic wines. From all accounts they, like many peasant populations, continued stolidly to cultivate the crops on which they depended, and it appears that they produced many a jar of illicit wine before the imperial decree was rescinded, under the Emperor Probus, 200 years later. Indeed, it seems highly unlikely that wine making could have been banned on this huge scale, especially while the Roman armies were moving throughout the vast empire. It was through the Rhône Valley that Caesar's legions had marched en route for the invasion of Britain, and the area was on the direct road taken by the imperial couriers going to all the northern provinces.

The Dark Ages

The sacking of Rome by the Vandals in A.D. 455 was the ultimate defeat of the Roman Empire by the barbarians, who had in fact been invading in increasing numbers during previous years. By the fifth century, France had been completely overrun by the Franks, the Germanic tribe that gave their name to the whole country. These were rightly known as the dark ages: Provence was a battle area for several centuries, the Saracens attacking in the eighth century and the Vikings a little later; they arrived through the Straits of Gibraltar and are supposed to have invaded the region even as far north as the Hermitage vineyards. The only places where any sort of culture was maintained were the religious establishments and there were plenty of these, again because of the convenience of the route from Rome to the north of France. Monasteries and, to a lesser extent, convents served as local hospitals and schools. They accommodated travellers of all kinds and of course trained those who would travel to other regions to set up more foundations.

This, according to records, was when some of the Rhône vineyards that are well known today were established. A religious house needed to be independent and surviving diagrams indicate that a vineyard, as well as herb and market gardens, fishponds and, sometimes, grazing for cattle, normally formed part of the overall layout. It was monks who cultivated vineyards in the Côtes du Ventoux, and Charlemagne (742–814) is reported to have halted his army at Cornas so as to approve the current vintage; he was certainly interested in vines and wine, so this seems probable.

As early as the twelfth century, the name of 'Châteauneuf' (*Novum castrum*—the new encampment) is to be found in documents of the period; the area came under the jurisdiction of the Bishop of Avignon. At the end of the twelfth century, the Knights Templars installed themselves near this 'Château' and fortified their holding so as to reinforce the episcopal castle. They extended the area they owned and, as in many of their other holdings, built a church and began to cultivate their own vineyards.

The Kingdom of Provence had been established in the middle of the ninth century. The region, now more settled, was much frequented by the troubadour poets; their lyrics, in the language of Provence, ranged from the devotional, through mannered compliments of courtly love, to dance songs and robust secular verses. Some of these troubadours were in fact of noble birth (the first of them was William IX, Duke of Aquitaine) and their influence was definitely a civilising one. Incidentally, the term 'Langue d'Oc', which then began to be used in Provence, derives from the fact that the Provençal word for 'Yes' was 'Oc', whereas the medieval word used in the rest of France was 'Oïl'—which became 'Oui'. So there was a sharp difference between the Langue d'Oc of the south and the Langue d'Oïl of the other regions.

Early in the thirteenth century, however, much of the civilisation of Provence was destroyed in the Albigensian

Crusade—bitter wars which were waged between the established church (with the future Saint Dominic a powerful influence) and the Albigensian heretics. Despite a savage defence, Avignon itself was taken. One of the leaders in the fight was a Frenchman, Simon de Montfort, whose son of the same name became so important in English history and is sometimes referred to as the 'father of the House of Commons'.

The Seat of the Papacy

One of the most notable events in the history of this area was when Avignon actually became the seat of the papacy in the fourteenth century.

It is thought possible that Christianity first arrived in Provence from the east and, therefore, it would have stemmed from the eastern rather than the western church. But progress was slow at the outset: André Maurois (1885–1967), the well-known French writer, reckoned that it took one hundred years to convert the inhabitants of the 250 miles of the Rhône Valley up to Lyon! The martyrs of Vienne and Lyon suffered in the arena (or were beheaded if of Roman citizenship) as late as A.D. 177. However, the area eventually became an important centre of Christianity; the Museum of Christian Art in Arles is world famous, and the Synod of Arles in A.D. 314 was one of the first great councils of the church, being attended by, among others, the bishops of London, York and possibly Lincoln.

In 1309 Philippe le Bel, King of France, had a serious dispute over taxes with Pope Boniface VIII; when this pope died, the King managed to get his own nominee, the Archbishop of Bordeaux (which then belonged to the English crown) elected as Pope Clément V. It was he who set up his court at Avignon instead of in Rome. Clément was definitely a man of wine—his parting gift to his flock was his own vineyard in the Graves, hence to this day its name is Pape Clément. Pope John XXII, successor to Clément, restored the 'Châteauneuf', enlarging the building so that it could house the entire pontifical court. He used it as a summer residence. Around it an estate was laid out, the wines and olive oil produced here becoming famous—and profitable. John XXII was in fact the creator of the viticulture which, eventually, transformed the whole aspect of the valley at this point and also the surrounding slopes. Indeed, he was not above commandeering other vineyards—including those of the Côtes du Ventoux—to provide for his court at Avignon, as he had 240 constant attendants, laity as well as clerics, to feed; visitors to his palace reported on the "bankers, money changers, tables loaded with gold and clerks weighing and counting out florins". When John died, his wealth was enormous. Possibly because of the large-scale building generally undertaken (the town had been burned in the riots at the death of Clément), there were also a number of lime kilns in the vicinity, earning for Châteauneuf the nickname 'Calcernier', a term that recurs as recently as the nineteenth century.

Pope Benedict XII, 'the White Cardinal' (because he continued to wear the white robes of the Cistercians), was a baker's son, the nephew of John XXII. He actually tore down much of the previous work on the papal palace, planning something massive and remarkable, but he did little for the Châteauneuf itself except to continue working the estate. Apparently he enjoyed the good things of life, for a Dominican contemporary describes him as '*potator egregius*', which might be translated as 'a notable drinker'. The poet Petrarch, so much associated with Avignon, relates that in addition to being "weighed down by age and wine", Benedict greatly appreciated the eels of Lake Bolsena, a notable delicacy. Petrarch, who did not like this Pope (he had hoped that Benedict would bring the papacy back to Rome), wrote of the great new Palace at Avignon " . . . in New Babylon we build towers both useless and absurd".

Benedict's successor, Clément VI, was known as 'the Magnificent'. He bought Avignon from Johanna, the Countess of Provence, in 1348 and the town and surroundings did not return to France for four centuries. Countess Johanna, thought to have had a hand in the assassination of her husband, the King of Naples, had been obliged to flee from avenging forces. Her property deal with the Pope was part of the price of her pardon.

Clément inaugurated a sumptuous epoch for Avignon and Châteauneuf and stocked up the now vast cellars of the papal palace. One of his banquets, described by a guest, featured a wine fountain which was brought in after the fifth course. From this flowed five different wines—those of the Rhine, Burgundy, St. Pourçain, La Rochelle (at that time a vineyard of importance) and, naturally, Provence.

The famous Courts of Love, started in the twelfth century, flourished in Provence at this time. One was held regularly at Aix, but moved to Signe and Pierrefeu in the winter; another was held in the winter at Avignon. The local great ladies presided and, although the days of the real troubadours were now past, the courts encouraged artists, musicians and poets, provided entertainment in the form of dialogues between men and women and, one might almost suggest, acted as a type of finishing school for many of the sons and daughters of the nobility who were sent away from home to be 'polished' and taught worldly manners.

When Innocent VI became Pope in 1353 he attempted to make good both the debts and shortcomings of his predecessor and his life seems to have been simple and upright; but for his ill health it is likely that he would have brought the papacy back to Rome. Urban V, 'the monk Pope' (he was a Benedictine), succeeded in 1362 and frugal life became the rule. Against the wishes of both the College of Cardinals and the King of France, he left Avignon for two years, returning shortly before his death.

Under Gregory XI Châteauneuf again flourished, but with his passing in 1377 the Great Schism in the Catholic Church began. It was to last thirty-nine years (1378–1417), with an 'Anti-Pope' established at Avignon in opposition to the Pope at Rome—both, needless to say, damning and excommunicating each other. At the beginning of the fifteenth century Benedict XIII, an Anti-Pope, was short of money so he pledged various territories, including Châteauneuf, as security for a loan; this pledge unfortunately fell into the hands of an unscrupulous adventurer, who ravaged the district under the pretence of reimbursing himself. However, during the reigns of the seven popes and two anti-popes who ruled from Avignon, the city benefited from the lavish patronage bestowed by the nobility on architects, painters and craftsmen.

The fifteenth century brought peace and prosperity to Provence, especially under the rule of René d'Anjou, who became Count of Provence and who is often referred to as '*le bon roi René*'; it was his nephew who bequeathed Provence to King Louis XI of France, after which the region's history is included with that of France.

The wines, however, retained their individual popularity: Louis XIII's table served only the wine of the royal holding, Clos de Tournon, in addition to the King's other vineyards at Beaune and Chenôve. Henri II kept Tournon wine for his personal use and the poet Ronsard also admired it. Local pride and, at various times, royal and papal patronage had created many legends about the Rhône Valley wines—God, the growers asserted, had favoured them by enabling them to make wines similar to that of the first miracle, when Jesus turned the water into wine at the marriage of Cana!

The Wars of Religion

During the sixteenth and seventeenth centuries the Wars of Religion in France, fought between the Huguenots (French Protestants) and Catholics, caused much destruction in the Rhône Valley. For its protection Châteauneuf was joined to the See of Avignon, but in 1561 the Calvinists descended on Châteauneuf, whose inhabitants temporarily abandoned the locality, and both the Church and Château were destroyed, leaving only the keep and a large ruined wall as a reminder of what had been. Montélimar was besieged and taken by the Protestants, who also pillaged Vienne and much of the region around Cairanne. With its fortress and position of great strategic value (it had been fortified by the Templars), Cairanne changed hands several times during the bitter fighting. When peace returned, the inhabitants left the high village and established themselves on lower ground, concentrating on cultivating their vineyards.

Finally, in 1598 Henry of Navarre granted the Huguenots religious freedom by the Edict of Nantes, and peace was restored. Ordinary life returned to the region, and Louis XIII was able to give the city of Montélimar to the Princes of Monaco—the Grimaldi family—who held it until the French Revolution. However, in 1643 Louis XIV ascended the throne of France and the Huguenots were once again a persecuted minority. With his revocation of the Edict of Nantes in 1685 many French Protestants were driven abroad. The reign of Louis XIV, splendid in many ways, was not necessarily so to those who endured the wars, plagues and social problems of the time. The population of Vienne, for example, declined from 20,000 to a mere 6,000.

The House of Orange

Travellers who wonder about the possible connection between the city of Orange and 'William of Orange' (King William III) are unlikely to find much helpful information in French books. But in fact the link is direct. Orange was an important Roman city which, by 1174, had become a principality that passed in marriage to Bertrand des Baux; in 1393 Marie des Baux, the last heiress, married John of Châlons, and in the sixteenth century their descendant Philibert of Orange-Châlons received a number of holdings in the Netherlands as a reward for his loyalty to the Emperor Charles V. Philibert died childless and was succeeded by his nephew Henry, son of the Count of Nassau, who was also a much favoured servant of the Emperor. When Henry died, he willed his titles and possessions to his first cousin, William, who had already inherited the German estates of his father. This William, who was only eleven years old when he became the Prince of Orange-Nassau, was the famous 'William the Silent' who founded the Dutch Republic. His grandson, William II, married Mary (daughter of Charles I of England) in 1641 and their child was the William III who, with his wife (also named Mary, and the daughter of James II), came to reign in England after the last Stuart monarch had fled.

After William's death there were many claimants to the Orange title but, at the Peace of Utrecht in 1713, Louis XIV acquired it—compensating other claimants with various rewards. He gave Orange to the then Lieutenant-Governor of Provence, the Comte de Grignan—another important literary event for Provence, for the Comte's third wife was the daughter of the Marquise de Sévigné (1626–1696), one of the most famous letter writers of all time. Madame de Sévigné's letters to her daughter at Grignan convey all the gossip of Paris but she often came to stay in Provence, where she delighted in the superb view from the terrace of the château and enjoyed the delicious food and the local wines. She died and was buried at Grignan, where tourists may still view parts of the château, including her room. The magnificent site is certainly worth seeing.

In 1719 Avignon, which until then had been administered by a Papal Legate, was formally reunited with France.

The Revolution and Recent History

During the reigns of Louis XV (1715–1774) and his son Louis XVI (1774–1789) the French royal family fell into disrepute, culminating in the French Revolution of 1789. This passed relatively peacefully in the Rhône region, but the Archbishopric was transferred to Lyon. However, the Rhône Valley suffered civil disturbances when, in 1792, the National Convention of the would-be reformers, abolishing royalty and proclaiming a new republic, was resisted by Lyon. This city had been of great commercial importance since medieval times—the first Foire de Lyon had been held in 1419 and, in 1449, the King granted Lyon the monopoly for the sale of silk throughout the whole of France. Suppressing the Lyonnais, who were understandably by no means anti-royalist, caused a true reign of terror in the region before peace could be restored.

During the nineteenth century many well-known people visited the Rhône Valley, including large numbers of British on cultural tours to Italy. There are numerous accounts by French writers: Alphonse Daudet (1840–1897) created a special type of character, in his *Tartarin* books, as well as describing the region in *Lettres de Mon Moulin*. George Sand and Alfred de Musset stopped at Pont Saint Esprit with Stendhal when en route for Italy and Stendhal got tipsy; Victor Hugo, in his novel *Les Misérables* (1862) describes how, at a reception given by M. Myriel for Jean Valjean, some of the wine of Tournon was sparingly served, in addition to *vin ordinaire*, because it was expensive—and, presumably, good. But the greatest of local writers must be the poet Frédéric Mistral (1830–1914); he spent most of his life in Provence, revived the use of Provençal as a language—his poem *Mirèio* is written in it—and used his 1905 Nobel Prize for Literature to enlarge the Museum Arlaten at Arles.

During the nineteenth century the wines of the Rhône increased in popularity in markets outside the region and methods of production improved. But in 1865 the aphis *phylloxera vastatrix* struck, first at Roquemaure and a year later at Châteauneuf-du-Pape, devastating the vineyards. This aphis, coming from the U.S., wiped out many European vineyards before it was found that, by grafting native stock onto American roots, which by then were resistant to the insect, the pest could be brought under control. But two-thirds of all the Rhône vineyards were destroyed before this discovery was made and action could be taken.

In World War I the Rhône vineyards, like all those of France, suffered from shortage of manpower; old men, women and children had to go and pick at vintage time and make and care for the wines. After the war, there was the long period of effort to produce quality Rhône wines and the introduction of the various *appellations* (see page 60). This continued after World War II and, indeed, still goes on.

World War II brought other grievous problems. Vienne was occupied by the Germans in 1940 and, on November 11th 1942, Provence was invaded by them. The region was ideal for the activities of the underground Résistance and large numbers of young men, who would otherwise have been deported for forced labour elsewhere, took to the '*maquis*' or countryside. Travellers who go off the beaten track will find many memorials to the brave men and women who gave their lives in the cause of freedom; this proud Valley is both tough and passionate, so commemorative tablets often do not bear the usual 'Died for their country' but 'Brutally murdered'.

In the vineyards, labour was short and chemicals to protect both the vines and other food crops were difficult, often impossible, to obtain. Although all crops suffer at such a time, it will be appreciated that vines, which need several years to reach maturity, require year-round attention (see pages 29 to 33). Even when they do yield of their best, neglect or ill-treatment can damage them in the long-term.

At the end of August 1944 the Allied forces landed on the south coast. Aided by the Résistance fighters they cleared Provence and, eventually, the entire Valley, fortunately without any damage to the vineyards. American and French troops liberated Vienne on September 1st, 1944. The final outrage of the war was the blowing up of the keep of Châteauneuf by the Germans, when they were in retreat from the Allied armies.

Since that unhappy time the region has developed enormously, and its wines have gone from strength to strength. Indeed, it is probably true to say that Rhône wines now receive more attention from the outside world than at any other period of their history—and, increasingly, more and more drinkers are discovering how rightly they deserve their reputation!

3
The Vines and the Wines they make

The production of wine is a combination of many factors: the most vital of these are the ripeness of the crop and the ability of the vintner to use his skill in producing the best possible results by careful vinification and maturation of his production.

There are many different ways of making wine, just as there are many choices before the grower. These start with the planning of the vineyard, the decision of whether he wishes to make red, white or rosé wines and, most important of all, what mixture of vine varieties he will plant in these vineyards. The vine varieties in most areas of France are few, but in the Rhône Valley the selection of permitted varieties is enormous, so the individual choice of the vintner plays a vital part in deciding on the quality of the wine which will finally be made. Expert advice, thanks to modern technological research, is readily available, so that it is possible to equate soil types, root stocks and vine varieties with each other. Modern viticultural methods can produce certain successes in the vineyard and, with four or five years' wait before the first real crop of grapes from which good wine can be made, the *vigneron* must have this expert advice. Fortunately, one of the most famous oenological establishments is near to the Rhône wine area, at Montpellier. In addition, and at least partly because the variety of grapes and soils in the region is a challenge to growers, there is an established tradition of quality wine making.

The Grapes

A wide variety of vines is planted in the Rhône Valley. Each has its own special properties and characteristics. It is this variety which enables the local wine maker to marry one grape variety with another from the area so as to make a perfect blend for the type of wine he wishes to make.

Syrah

The Syrah grape (known in the Rhône as the Serine) has a long ancestry, but there is some controversy amongst French authorities as to its exact origin. Some claim that it was brought from Syracuse in Sicily before the dawn of the Christian era. Others think that the Crusaders brought it back to Europe from Shiraz in Persia, where it was cultivated. In support of the Syrah-Syracuse theory, it should be noted that the Greeks, who brought the wine vine to Provence around 600 B.C., had previously established both colonies and vineyards in Sicily.

The Syrah is one of the greatest black grapes of the Rhône. It gives body, vigour and colour to red wines, making them very aromatic and long-lived. Wines made largely from the Syrah require laying down for at least two or three years—and preferably more—before they are drunk. When the assertive nature of the Syrah is tempered by blending it with suitable white varieties, some of the world's finest wines are produced: when blended with the Viognier in the Côte Rôtie, with the Marsanne and Roussanne at Hermitage, and with several other varieties in Châteuneuf-du-Pape, some very great wines result.

Grenache

The main variety of the Grenache, a black grape, is of Spanish origin (Garnacha). It is essential for the productive vineyards of the southern Rhône area, and also those further south in the Midi. Ideal for cultivation on slopes, the Grenache produces wines with body, good alcoholic strength, firmness and a fine, deep red colour. They are especially enjoyable in their youth, as they are markedly fruity when young.

The Grenache blends extremely well with the Syrah, Mourvèdre and Cinsaut to produce excellent long-lived wines. Variations of the variety are the Grenache Rouge, Grenache Gris and Grenache Blanc.

Ugni Blanc

A white vine variety of Italian origin, this is planted in small quantities in the Rhône area. It is the main variety planted in Cognac, where it is known as the St. Émilion Charente. Its contribution to Rhône is its high acidity, which gives crispness.

Mourvèdre

This is an old Provençal variety of high quality, which grows well in the soils of many Rhône vineyards. It was disregarded for many years, but is now being planted again in many of the best sites. Mourvèdre makes wines which are ideal for blending and which age well, contributing a full, slightly soft and fragrant character. However, the Mourvèdre is a variety that is never left unblended.

TAILLE GUYOT *A system of cordon pruning*

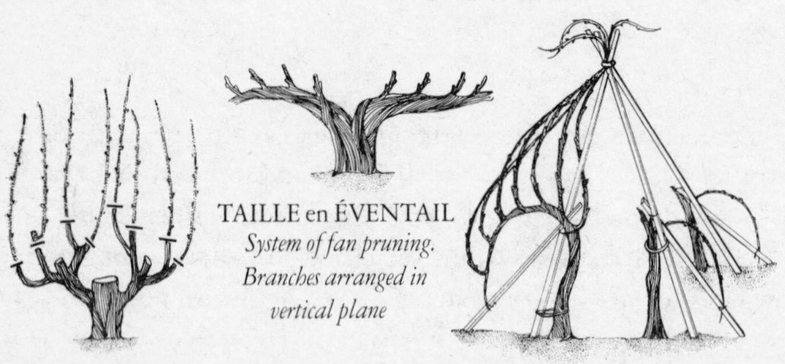

TAILLE GOBELET
Bush pruning

TAILLE de CÔTE-RÔTIE
The vines are trained together in groups

Methods of pruning vines in the Côtes-du-Rhône area

Bourboulenc

This is a vigorous variety of black grape which makes lighter wines than the Clairette, but with more freshness and staying power. Bourboulenc is ideal for blending, and is used in many of the most important Rhône wines.

Clairette

This is an excellent vine, yielding black grapes, which adapts well to poor soil. It produces light, elegant wines with good colour and staying power, and these characteristics are revealed while the wines are still young.

Viognier

This white grape produces delightful characteristic wines such as Condrieu and Château Grillet. Its characteristics are its special aromatic bouquet and its full, distinctive dryness. The Viognier is used in Côte Rôtie wines as a blender to temper the fire of the Syrah.

Marsanne and Roussanne (or Roussette)

These are the white varieties of grapes used in Hermitage, Crozes Hermitage and St. Péray. They produce full-bodied wines which are very fresh in their youth and which age gracefully into very fine dry wines. When used for the sparkling dry whites of St. Péray they produce highly-flavoured wines, but the varieties are too full in style to give elegance.

Carignan

This vine is well adapted to poor soil (it is widely used in many southern vineyards and in Spain). Wines made from its black grapes are well balanced and have good keeping qualities. It is an ideal blending partner to use with the Grenache, because it has an underlying powerful flavour, with a touch of sweetness. This partnership of the Grenache and the Carignan is perfect for making rosé.

Gamay

The grape of Beaujolais, this vine produces light, fruity wines of a brilliant red. It yields well in the small areas of the Rhône where it is planted.

Aligoté

This white-grape vine is best known for producing inexpensive Burgundy. The vine is hardy, and can therefore be grown at relatively high altitudes. The wines are pleasantly fresh and acidic when young, but they do not age particularly well.

Muscat (Muscat à petits grains)

This is a vine of Greek origin which produces wines that are powerfully scented. It produces dry wines in Alsace, but at Beaumes de Venise and Frontignan the grapes are fortified to produce sweet wines of an outstandingly 'grapey' smell and fruity taste.

Cinsaut (Cinsault)

This black grape produces quality red wines from stony soil—light, fruity, fine and elegant. They are delightful when young, but can also be excellent in 'long life' blends because of their sinewey character.

Other vines used in the area include the *Counoise, Picardan* and *Vaccarèse,* but these are nowadays planted in comparatively small proportions.

How the Wines are made

Red Wines

Generally, the red wines are prepared by fermenting the must (the freshly squeezed grape juice) together with the skins, pips and stalks. On arrival at the cellars the grapes are crushed between grooved rollers (this process is known as *foulage*), and the mash is then pumped into large vats and lightly sulphured. It is at this stage that the more delicate arts of vinification come to the fore, as this is the best time for blending the grapes from different vineyards and also from varying vine stocks.

The partial blend having been made (the final blend is made later, from several *cuvées* or vattings, as not all the grapes ripen and get picked at the same time), the mash is allowed to ferment. Fermentation is caused by the yeasts present in the grape skins coming into contact with the sugar in the grape juice; this interaction produces alcohol and carbon dioxide (CO_2). The temperature in the vats is kept, as far as possible, between 20°C and 30°C. Higher temperatures than 30°C produce a wine with less bouquet and finesse, and the danger of bacterial infection increases.

The fermentation, which normally takes place in large concrete- or glass-lined vats, must be extremely carefully controlled: temperature rises and bacterial infection must be avoided at all costs. The carbon dioxide that is produced by the fermentation bubbles its way to the surface, taking the pulp of skins and pips with it, and here they are exposed to the air. This layer (known as the 'hat' or *chapeau*) tends to float on the surface and it must be kept free from infections which would rapidly turn the wine to vinegar. Many methods are employed to keep the *chapeau* broken up and below the surface: some modern vats have submerged grids to keep the hat down. Similar results can be obtained by pumping wine up from underneath on to the top of the wine's surface, which effectively cools the wine at the same time. Extreme care is taken during this process, as with all work in cellars during the fermentation period, so as to avoid excessive concentration of carbon dioxide in the air, as this could cause asphyxiation of the cellarmen. Visitors who lean over to see what is going on in the vat are usually warned not to inhale the gas, as it could give them an upset stomach.

In an extremely hot and dry year, when the grapes are small, fermentation is carried out without the stalks and pips being left in the must as their presence would increase the tannin content too much. This would make the wine hard, and it would take years to come round. Immediately after their arrival at the cellars, the grapes are either pumped to or allowed to drop into an extractor machine, which rejects the stalks and leaves the skin and must. This process is known as *égrappage*. Fermentation then proceeds as usual.

In some years it is necessary to adjust the final tannin content so as to obtain a well balanced wine. This can only be done by preparing a special *cuvée* or vatting, by mixing some grapes left on their stalks with those already without stalks (*égrappé*), a procedure which requires expert judgement for success.

After the end of fermentation, which may take two weeks or much longer, depending entirely on the individual maker, the wine remains in the fermentation vat for several days (sometimes weeks or even months). After this it is racked (drawn off any deposit) into large wooden vats or individual hogsheads, where it remains for maturing for at least six months. This period of maturation in wood is essential for stabilising the wine before it is bottled, in order to ensure that it matures gently once in bottle.

Most fine red wines benefit from long storage in wood casks and the Rhône vintners follow the pattern established in other French vineyard areas. In some cellars small hogsheads (containing 210–225 litres) are used, while in others they have giant casks holding several thousand litres. The smaller the cask, the higher the proportion of wine that is in actual contact with the wood—and in contact with air and tannin, both of which allow physical and chemical changes to take place.

The remaining mash from the vat is then pressed by hydraulic presses. The wine from this process is called *vin de presse* and it is usually much harsher than the wine produced from the drawn-off liquid, because its tannin content is considerably higher. It is used for domestic consumption by the workers and growers.

Depending upon the harvest, the period of maturation for the wines in wood takes from fifteen months upwards, although the lighter reds may be bottled within twelve months of their harvest. During this time the casks are topped up frequently so as to replace the wine that has been lost by evaporation during the ageing process. This topping up is necessary in order to avoid spoilage of the wine, which would occur from its exposure to the air in the cask if its level were allowed to fall. The wine is racked four times a year (December, February, April and June) so as to take the wine off its sediment prior to bottling.

Bottling usually takes place after two years, just before vintage time, but it can be delayed for as much as seven years. This is necessary for the bigger red wines. When these are made according to traditional vinification, the rich full wines in the northern Rhône and those from certain favoured areas in the south, particularly Châteauneuf-du-Pape and Gigondas, improve enormously during their second year in cask; they continue to improve in their third and fourth years, too, provided the cellar conditions remain perfect as regards temperature and humidity. The finest Châteauneuf-du-Pape vintages used to be matured in cask for four to six years. But maturation is an additional expense. For example, during maturation approximately 10 per cent of the wine is lost in the first year and 5 per cent in the second year, simply by evaporation. So the long-term ageing that many people say is a good idea is not always an economic possibility, however desirable in an ideal world.

After ageing the wine is then fined with a gelatine. This means that any particles still suspended in the wine are attracted to the substance that has been added, so that the particles can then be removed together with the fining substance and leave the wine clear. After fining the wine may also be filtered before it is bottled.

Unfortunately, financial pressures on growers are such that they are inclined nowadays to produce wines for early maturation rather than those suited to the traditional lengthy maturing in wood. But, generally speaking, these lighter fruitier red wines are popular on both sides of the Atlantic. They are fruity, full of flavour, easy to understand and enjoy and, as wine is a commodity that the makers and shippers have to sell, their popularity is an important consideration for the producers. However, it is regrettable that traditional methods have had to be changed for financial reasons, and the possible danger of the traditional characters and flavours of Rhône reds being forgotten must not be overlooked. Wine lovers who cherish the old-style reds must be prepared to pay more for them.

Macération Carbonique

A now well-proven modern method of producing red wines is *macération carbonique*, a process that has been used most successfully for many fine Beaujolais *Crûs*. The grapes, while still on their stalks, are placed in a cement vat, which is sealed. Partial fermentation of the must is obtained by self-pressing of the grapes, which occurs simply because of their own weight pressing down upon them. This self-pressing produces CO_2 which, under pressure, macerates or acts on the grapes, without allowing further fermentation. Between 18 and 22 days later the pressure is carefully released, the mash is passed into the hydraulic presses and the resulting must is pumped into fresh vats. The normal alcoholic fermentation then proceeds smoothly at this stage, taking from seven to ten days.

This technique results in an improved and accelerated fermentation, and it also completes the malo-lactic fermentation. In this secondary fermentation, the malic acid in the new wine is converted into lactic acid. Contact of the must with the skins at normal temperature prior to fermentation gives more ultimate bouquet to a *cuvée* than would occur under normal fermentation—that is, after the grapes had been stripped from their stalks prior to vatting. This method has now been carried out for long enough to prove that *macération carbonique* wines stand the test of time very well. Their further treatment is identical to the method described previously for red wines, but *macération carbonique* wines can be bottled within a year of their vintage and they will be drinkable soon afterwards. There are many opinions about this new method, some thinking that it should be combined with normal wine-making techniques while others enjoy these delicious youthful wines as they are, and are not concerned about long-term maturation.

White Wines

For making these, the grapes are brought to the press house immediately after picking. Here the must or grape juice is obtained by pressing the grapes, stalks and branches together; there is no separation of the fruit and tannin-containing materials. The must is run into previously sulphured hogsheads and there allowed to settle, while the unwanted solids from the grapes accumulate at the bottom of the cask—these are the lees. The bright, clean must is then racked off into clean casks leaving the deposit behind. The new casks are not filled right to the top. Pure yeast is added and fermentation allowed to proceed. The cask is sealed with a special glass or plastic bung, which allows the carbon dioxide generated during fermentation to escape freely without any cellar air being drawn into the cask.

The fermentation procedure varies from maker to maker, but the wine is generally racked off the lees (the sediment— insoluble by-products of fermentation and dead yeasts) into a clean, slightly sulphured cask soon after termination, or when the fermentation is finished. In exceptional vintages, with musts of a high sugar content (giving wines of high alcoholic strength), the fermentation may be slow and difficult.

The process of racking is repeated several times during the time that the wine is kept in cask. Before bottling the wine is sometimes fined with bentonite, sand, or egg white and/or gelatine. This is to ensure that the wine is 'star-bright' when it is bottled.

At the time of writing, many producers still wait for up to two years before bottling their white wines; however, experience has shown that during the second year in cask the wines can lose their finesse and bouquet, darken appreciably in colour and even maderise, which makes them less palatable for modern style drinking habits. Forward-thinking *vignerons* (producers) now bottle their white wines after only one year in cask, sometimes even within nine or twelve months of the harvest. This results in a drier product, far more appreciated by today's clientèle. Many growers also now prefer to age their white wines in stainless steel or other inert containers, rather than in wood, as the wines stabilise better in such airtight containers. When white wines are wood aged—even for a year—it is very important that all precautions are taken to prevent excessive contact with air, as this darkens the wine and can affect the flavour.

Rosé Wines

The production of rosé wines begins in exactly the same way as for red wines: fermentation is allowed to continue with the grape must (now partially alcohol) in contact with the skins. It is the alcohol which removes the colouring matter from the skin layers of the black grapes, and after 24 hours (sometimes longer, depending upon the temperature) the fermenting grape juice has usually attained a pleasant pink colour. When the colour is judged sufficient by the maker, the whole mass is passed to the wine presses and the partially-fermented grape juice is separated completely from the skins and residues. From this point on the wine's treatment follows the same pattern as that for white wine.

"Traditional" Clairette de Die

The harvested grapes are pressed as soon as they arrive at the cellars, and the grape juice is then immediately cooled to 0°C. Most of the skins, pulp, etc. are precipitated (separated from the liquid) and the must is then filtered through kieselguhr (diatomite) so as to rid it completely of any impurities. The fermentation which follows is carried out over a very long period at very low temperatures. This keeps the sugar content at the high levels which are needed to produce the second fermentation which is an essential part of the production of sparkling wine.

The wine is then given its second fermentation in bottle. This means that the process follows the Champagne method and this stage must continue for at least four months to entitle the end product to the *appellation* 'Clairette de Die "tradition" '. But, in contrast to the Champagne process, the wine is then removed from its first bottle and is filtered at low temperature by counter pressure of inert gas (in order to avoid any loss of the carbon dioxide which gives the wine its fizz). Finally, it is bottled in the traditional pressure-resistant bottle and is stoppered with a cork secured with the traditional twisted wires.

Vins de Café

The Rhône Valley produces very large quantities of light, fruity wines known as '*vins de café*'. These come in particular from the Ventoux area, where more than half of the production is for wines of this type. After arrival at the presshouse the grapes are de-stalked and crushed. The must (grape juice) is sulphured, cleansed and allowed to ferment: fermentation is generally fast in this warm southern climate. A relatively short fermentation in the presence of the skins produces a light red wine with a lovely flavour but without the tannin which normally gives red wines their staying power. After stabilising (only for about 9 months), the wines are ready for consumption and are designed for sale as carafe (open) wines in cafés and restaurants throughout France.

The vigneron's year in Châteauneuf-du-Pape

Baron le Roy, son of the originator of *Appellation Controlée* (p.89) and owner of one of the finest and most famous estates, gave me details of his annual routine. During the summer the work of the grower increases, culminating in the harvesting of his crop or vintage. Meanwhile, constant vigil must be maintained against infection of the vines and their fruit. The autumn is the most critical period and the *vigneron* works around the clock ensuring that his wines are fermenting at the correct temperature and that they will not become liable to bacterial infection. After the first racking into wood at the end of the fermentation, the *vigneron* can relax and look back on his work—one hopes with satisfaction.

Vineyard Work

The main work consists of light ploughing which keeps the soil mobile and free from weeds. Pests and fungi are controlled by chemical means.

The most important diseases and pests which have to be fought include:

Oïdium, a powdery mildew which attacks both vine and fruit. The grape skins harden, growth ceases and the berries drop. This can be cured by dusting the vines with sulphur or solutions of sulphur.

Mildew, caused by damp and humidity, which causes discoloration of leaves and berries. It can be prevented by spraying with copper-containing solutions.

Grey mould, a fungus affecting the berries, which stops their growth, decolorising and shrivelling the berries. It can be combated with modern chemical sprays.

Red spiders, which tear the leaves along the veins, and

Caterpillars, which eat the buds, the blossom and the berries. These last two can both be combated with various sprays.

Finally, and perhaps most hazardous of all, as there is no way to control her, there is Nature. Spring frosts can destroy young shoots and autumn frosts cause leaves to fall. Freak storms can ruin a harvest (in June 1964 the vineyards of Châteauneuf-du-Pape suffered from severe hailstorms followed by floods which destroyed 2,000 acres of vines), as can insufficient rain or sunshine, and the Rhône Valley always has the Mistral to contend with.

Vineyard work is dependant on the temperature and level of humidity. In normal years, up to nine spraying treatments are carried out, but in a wet season the vineyards may require more than double this. Regular spraying is with 'Bordeaux mixture'—a combination of copper sulphate, lime and water.

A month-by-month breakdown of the vineyard cycle:

October

Vintage time—the fruit of the summer sunshine. Picking is carefully controlled, with the white grapes being collected first by a small team. The black grapes are picked in sequence: Syrah first, then Grenache, followed by Mourvèdre and other varieties.

Picking follows a strict routine—during the first 'tour' through the vineyard only the more mature grapes are harvested, but the second 'tour' is selective, a distinction being made between grapes which have matured in the meantime and those which are only suitable for *vin ordinaire*. A third 'tour' collects the remaining grapes, which are also for making *vin ordinaire*.

The vinification proceeds as described on page 22. However in Châteauneuf-du-Pape, with its warm to hot autumns, it is especially important to keep the vat temperature, where fermentation proceeds, below 28/30°C. This is a very busy time for the cellar staff, and they may have to cool the vats with water sprays.

November

The vintage of the year before is racked into clean casks, so as to remove the lees.

The main fermentation of the new wine should have finished and the temperature in the cellars will have dropped as winter approaches. The malo-lactic fermentation is then encouraged, by warming the cellars to a temperature of 23/24°C.

Vineyard staff make good any damage and uproot any dead vines, at the same time preparing the soil for new plants. This is a good time to spread manure.

The first frosts come and, towards the middle of the month, a start is made on pruning the vines.

December

The new wines must be racked off their heavy lees into clean casks or vats.

The vineyard work of pruning and soil preparation continues.

January

Even during this cold period pruning must continue, as it must be finished before the end of March. The average worker can prune up to 400 vines per day.

Bottling of the previous vintage is begun, depending on the development of the wine in cask. Various *cuvées* are blended in order to produce the best results and as uniform a wine as possible.

February

Bottling continues. Casks must be topped up to avoid oxidation or bacterial spoilage.

Pruning continues in the vineyard.

March

Pruning is finished. New vines are planted after the middle of the month to replace dead ones. *Decavaillonage*—the drawing back of the soil which was placed around the vine bases to protect the roots from frost—is now carried out so as to expose the vines to the sun and warmth of spring. The soil is aerated by ploughing. Wires for training the Syrah are replaced.

April

The second racking of the new wine into clean casks for maturation takes place. All casks are topped up regularly.

Vineyard work continues: the Syrah vines are attached to supporting wires, and the other vines receive their first treatment against red spiders and mildew.

May

Racking the new wine must be finished before the 15th, as should the bottling of old wines.

In the vineyard, ploughing continues. This is normally carried out in a right-angled direction (*croise*). Treatment of the vines against mildew is essential now.

June

Flowering should occur—it is vital that there is warm weather at this time for the setting of the fruit. Ploughing goes on and, in the second week of the month, it is vital to treat the soil against worms. If necessary, treatment against mildew continues.

Vines exposed to the Mistral require staking and support, wild shoots must be removed, and any excess buds should be cut off.

July

The final bottling takes place before the annual holiday. The new wines are given their third racking at the end of the month.

In the vineyard, a final tilling takes place before the middle of the month and the arrival of the hot weather. Unwanted shoots are removed, while the best shoots are attached to wires for support.

By mid-month a final treatment against mildew and worms is given. Overproduction on young vines is prevented by pruning, and dead vines are removed.

August

All casks are topped up and the cellars prepared for visitors.

Anti-mildew treatments continue as and when necessary. The vineyards are kept tidy by ploughing, weeding and the removal of unwanted shoots.

September

The final racking before the harvest takes place. All casks are topped up and cellar equipment is thoroughly cleaned, ready to receive the new crop.

Now is the time to carry out regular checks on the maturity of the grapes, so as to decide when to start picking each variety.

Harvesting normally begins at the end of the month, and the cycle starts again.

The Vineyards

Côte Rôtie

From the north, the first of the more important Rhône vineyards is the Côte Rôtie. It clings to the hillsides to the south of Vienne

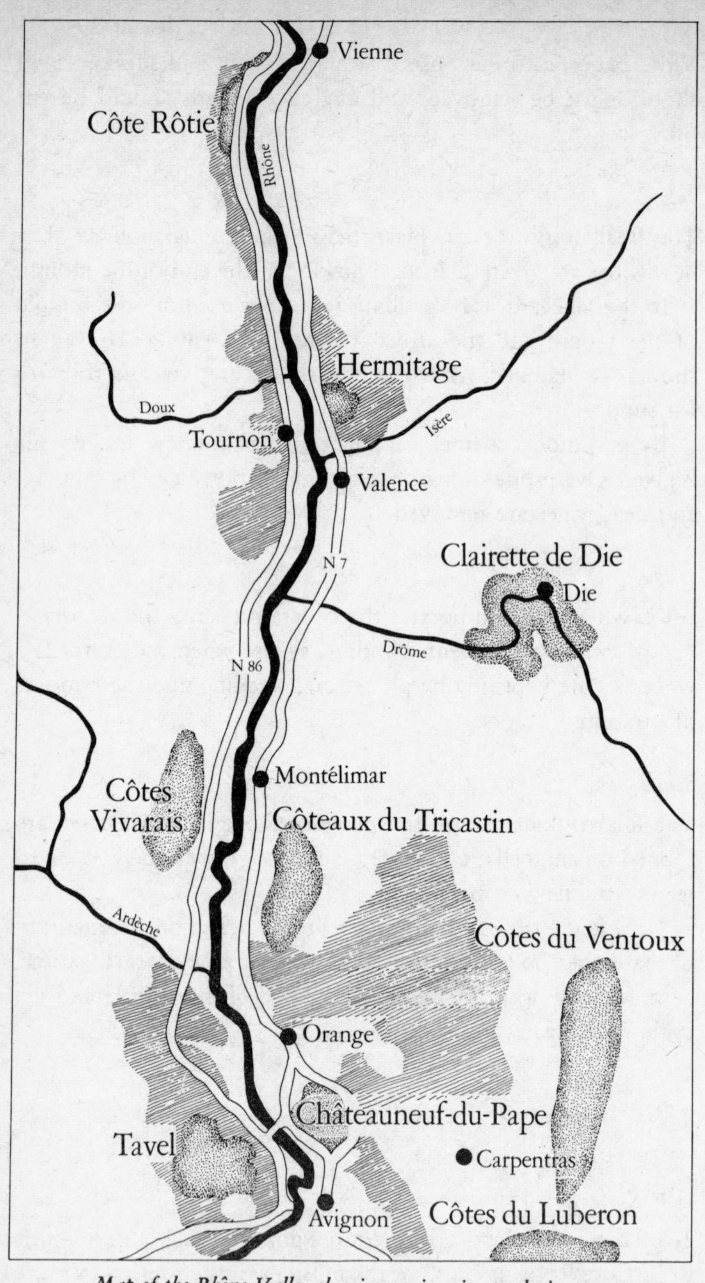

Map of the Rhône Valley showing main wine-producing areas

on the opposite side of the river, above the village of Ampuis, and stretches into Tupin and Semons.

The vines of Côte Rôtie almost hang from the steep sun-roasted slopes, which are stoutly buttressed by stone walls. The slopes are divided into small terraces, some so tiny that they contain only one or two vines. The retaining walls are known as *cheys* or *murgeys*, and without them cultivation, already backbreaking, would be virtually impossible. The severity of the slopes makes mechanisation impossible and human labour most arduous, so hard work the whole year round is the rule. Much of the work is carried out with the *bigot*, a two-pronged hoe, and often the eroded soil, which is sandy and stony, has to be carried back uphill.

But in spite of these difficulties Côte Rôtie produces one of the oldest, greatest and most aristocratic wines of the Côtes-du-Rhône, more delicate and less 'powerful' than those of Châteauneuf-du-Pape. The vineyards extend in a green ribbon two miles long, high above the Rhône. A fortunate bend in the river gives them the advantage of a south-east exposure, and the baking sun that beats down for most of the summer brings the grapes to an early harvest.

Côte Rôtie has an ancient and noble lineage. We know from the works of the Latin writers that the Romans loved the wines from these hillsides. The proconsuls at Vienne served it at their banquets and sent presents of it in goatskin containers to Rome in hope of favours to come. And it was here, too, that they made their *vinum picatum*, so called because the black 'picata' grape from which it was pressed yielded a slight but apparently unmistakable taste of pitch. Pliny the Elder and Martial among the Latins, and Plutarch, the Greek biographer, all mention this. Pliny's references are not entirely complimentary, for he records that its high reputation in its homeland was not always upheld elsewhere.

I have often wondered, when reading of early references to wine, how many vintages the authors had actually tasted on which to base their views. It is rather surprising to learn that Pliny (first century A.D.) described 90 varieties of vines and listed

50 types of wine. So the early connoisseurs did have a fairly wide choice, but how good it really was we shall never know.

By the terms of the *appellation* laws introduced in 1940, Côte Rôtie is produced from two vines—80 per cent Syrah (black) and 20 per cent Viognier (white); these proportions yield a finely-perfumed, full-bodied yet subtle red wine with a touch of purple in its rich colour, and a flavour suggestive of raspberries. One of its admirers (a leading grower) describes it as a "wine of quality, a lord without arrogance or false pretension, but proud of a long history which has opened to it all the most famous cellars."

Côte Rôtie keeps well, sometimes requiring twelve years to mature (five of them as a rule in the wood), and it retains its goodness for up to fifteen years, in some cases much longer. However, modern red wine techniques tend to bring the wine forward more rapidly, and it is generally bottled two years after its vintage.

The *appellation* minimum strength is 10 per cent alcohol, but the better wines generally exceed this figure, according to the year and the weather. There is also a limitation on the output per hectare, but I am sure it is easy to comply with this restriction on the steep terraced hillsides of the Côte Rôtie, where in places the vines prosper only because the granite rock has had to be smashed up with picks to give the vine roots a foothold. Two of the best known slopes of Côte Rôtie are named the Côte Brune and the Côte Blonde, the latter being just south of the other. The legend is that, centuries ago, the Seigneur of Ampuis had two daughters, a blonde and a brunette, to each of whom he gave one of the vineyards as dowry. The soil, as it happens, matches the names: that of Côte Brune is a brownish clay, while the other, being of a silico-calcareous nature, has a lighter appearance.

It is no surprise that, from their different soils, the blonde and her darker sister make wines that show marked differences in their qualities. Côte Brune is the more full-bodied, takes time to reach maturity and lasts well. The Côte Blonde is softer, lighter and fruitier, comes of age more quickly and is said not to be so reliable as it gets older.

There is, however, nothing fierce or fickle in the end product, and the two charming sisters carry their differing qualities to the blending cellars, where they are combined in a delectable wine that sometimes comes on the market labelled 'Brune et Blonde'. Most of the wine, however, is sold as 'Côte Rôtie', although in France some of these wines are sold with the individual site names.

Condrieu

Immediately south of the red wine slopes of Côte Rôtie is the smaller area of Condrieu, where only the Viognier grape is grown: consequently the yield is only of white wine. Here too the hillside is steep, calling for numerous retaining walls—from a distance the terrace resembles a staircase climbing to the sky, and the view from the top is fabulous. Work involves the sweat of the brow and again the pick is an indispensable tool.

Condrieu is made in various styles, according to the grower's choice: the traditional method produces full-bodied dry wines, whereas modern methods can yield a lighter and slightly sweeter vintage. Some wines are even *pétillant* or slightly sparkling (similar to young Moselle and the Portuguese *vinhos verdes*), and these are generally drunk during the winter and spring following the vintage. Wine making is carried out on an individual basis, and growers keep their secrets strictly to themselves (as they do in other parts of France). Condrieu wine is supposed to age well, but it loses most of its fruitiness in the process.

Fewer than twenty acres of Condrieu's rock soil is under these Viognier vines, so the output is limited. In an average year less than 2,000 gallons, or about 12,000 bottles, are produced. The area of Condrieu takes in three communes—Condrieu, Vérin and St. Michel.

Château Grillet

On the next hillside is a Lilliput among vineyards—Château

Grillet. There are barely three acres of it (under a single proprietor, M. Gachet) and even in a good year the yield from its Viognier vines is not more than 11,000 bottles, although as new vines are planted the production is increasing.

The estate is managed in the traditional manner, so that the wine is always full-bodied and dry, with a delicious flower-like bouquet; in its most delicate form it is reminiscent of violets. I was able during several visits to taste a range of eight vintages: I prefer the wines of lesser years, which show more finesse and bouquet, to those of magnificent vintages, which I think tend to be too full-bodied and lacking in elegance—a phenomenon to my mind similar to what occurs with the Sauvignon grape in Pouilly-Fumé on the Loire.

The vineyard of Château Grillet (incidentally, the smallest to have its own *appellation contrôlée*) shares the granitic soil of its neighbours, which is grey and gritty. The estate is in the two communes of Verin and St. Michel. Small walled terraces rise one above the other and hold no more than two rows of vines, sometimes only a few plants. Their southern exposure and the hot dry climate atone for the hard labour of cultivation. After the October harvest, the must (grape juice) undergoes a slow fermentation and remains on the lees (sediment) for weeks or even months; there have to be several rackings (drawings-off) to ensure perfect clarification of the wine, which generally has up to two years in wood and twice that time in bottle. (But I believe that a better wine would be obtained if it were racked immediately after fermentation and bottled in the spring of the following year.)

Château Grillet's scarcity and its renown have made it something of a connoisseur's wine. Several of the vintages I have tasted have not seemed to me to live up to their reputation, as the use of plastic corks seemingly aged the wine much too fast. This has long been changed, and since 1962 all bottles have been closed with cork. The 1962 vintage was full-bodied with a fine flowery flavour (possibly violets) but without outstanding bouquet. Comparison is never perfect but to me it seems nearest to a Grand Crû Chablis, with more body but less finesse and elegance.

Alexis Lichine in *Wines of France* says that this is considered the outstanding *vin du pays* of France, and Morton Shand (*A Book of French Wines*, Cape, 1928) found in its "floral May-blossom scent and flavour . . . a curious affinity with the genius of the Rhine". Thanks to Mr. Shand, Maurice Healy was lucky enough to drink a Château Grillet that was nearly 70 years old, and in *Stay Me With Flagons* (Michael Joseph, 1940) he reported of that bottle that "it appeared to be of a majesty greater than that attained by Chablis or any Burgundy except Montrachet." These compliments make it an intriguing wine, and motorists speeding south to the holiday coast might well stop in this pleasant and hospitable spot and try to acquire a bottle or even a glass of this local wine. Scarcity produces demand, and so Château Grillet is to be found in only three restaurants in the region (at a relatively high price) and in the homes of the proprietor's friends. A small quantity of every vintage is shipped to the U.K. and the U.S.A.

Tournon and Saint-Joseph

On the opposite side of the Rhône above Tournon, twin township of Tain, lie the vineyards of Saint-Joseph. The *appellation* Saint-Joseph does not apply to one village but to five, all situated in the area immediately around Tournon. The red and white wines produced in this area were formerly known by the generic term Côtes-du-Rhône, and were largely used for blending with those of other areas, but in 1956 the growers, thanks to improved vinicultural methods, gained their own *appellation contrôlée* and thus became entitled to market their wine under its own name. (This is not dissimilar in principle from a football team gaining promotion from one league to a higher one.) The wines, both white and red, are held to have the characteristics (in lesser form) of Côte Rôtie and Hermitage, and though they are little known outside their locality they have been consistently popular through the ages.

The *appellation* Saint-Joseph includes the communes of Glun, Lemps, Mauves, St. Jean-de-Muzols and Vion.

Hermitage

From among the long list of compliments paid to Hermitage it may be sufficient to recall that George Meredith praised it through one of his characters, and Professor George Saintbury (*Notes from a Cellar Book*, 1923) debated whether an 1846 Hermitage or a Romanée-Conti of 1858 was the greatest vintage he had ever known. Praise indeed! He drank the Hermitage when it was forty years old, and described it as "the manliest French wine I ever drank".

An age-old saying, well-known along the Côtes-du-Rhône, says "Plant the rugged vine on the slopes of the hillside, and the heart of the granite will bleed into your vine". At Hermitage it can bleed red and white, the red from the Syrah grape and the long-living white from the Roussanne and, above all, from the Marsanne.

The fifteenth century castle at Tournon, with the hill of Hermitage in the background

Taste and bouquet vary according to site and sun, while the 'bad-tempered' Mistral can also have distinct effects. This Midi wind does not blow as hard at Hermitage as it does further south, but when it whip-lashes with intensity it can break off bunches of grapes. Too much of it at harvest time may result in a sharp temperature rise and, therefore, increase the speed of fermentation. When this happens, great skill is required to counteract what might otherwise be harmful effects.

About 80 per cent of the wines are red. They have a ruby richness of colour with a suggestion of purple brilliance. They are generous and mellow with a raspberry-like flavour and bouquet; they keep well and, as with most Rhône wines, they are a superb accompaniment to such traditional dishes as are usually associated with Burgundy by the British.

The white Hermitage has a great reputation for longevity, and many authorities rate it among the notable white wines. Certainly in a good year this dry, pleasantly-perfumed beverage deserves that place. Some detect a touch of 'gun flint' in its aroma (is this a mythical phenomenon?) and attribute this to the stony nature of the soil. These stones were once on the bed of the Rhône in the far distant prehistoric times, when the river was still carving out the great valley through which it now flows. The white wines should be served well chilled but never iced, as that can spoil both the bouquet and the flavour.

Hardly known nowadays are the '*vins de paille*'—straw wines. These supposedly interesting wines are made from grapes which have been left to dry on straw mats for at least two months. The grapes can also be suspended in bunches for the same length of time. Golden in colour, the wine made from the artificially concentrated grape-juice is strong, but only small amounts have ever been produced. It has been described as 'wine of the sun, the perfumed sun!' However, I have not been able to trace any made here since 1913, and possibly those that may still be produced are solely for private consumption.

The Hermitage vineyards run for about five kilometres along the sunny shelf above the Rhône, and they are divided into two main sections: Crozes-Hermitage and l'Hermitage. The former vineyards (350 hectares) span the following communes: Serves, Erome, Gervans, Larnage, Mercurol, Chanos-Curson, Beaumont-Monteaux, La Roche de Glun, Pont de l'Isère, Crozes Hermitage and Tain l'Hermitage; l'Hermitage in the commune of Tain is barely 120 hectares. Most of the plots (or '*quartiers*' as they are called) are small, and the many owners mostly have a few plots scattered throughout the area. The variations of slope, sun and soil produce different characteristics in the wines, so that each owner can draw on several types of wine for blending: this is necessary in order to obtain a uniform product.

The wines of Crozes are less powerful and of a slightly less definite character than those of l'Hermitage, which has ideal exposure to the sun. Although the wines of the two sections are described as 'if not brothers then definitely first cousins', Crozes is less robust than l'Hermitage but not as elegant. Although the vines are the same, vineyard work for Crozes is less difficult than for the l'Hermitage.

The growers are always proud to tell of how in their grandfather's time Hermitage was sometimes used to 'stretch' Bordeaux vintages when that area had a lean year. During the same period Burgundy owed a similar debt to Châteauneuf-du-Pape.

Cornas

The town of Cornas, situated where the River Isère joins the Rhône, has been making red wine from the Syrah grape for a long time, and its history can be traced back at least to the ninth century A.D. The soil of the hill on which the vineyards are laid out originated from Alpine diluvium, which accounts for its stony nature. It reaches a height of nearly 800 feet and some slopes are at an angle of 45 degrees, which means kilometres of soil-retaining walls and continual hard work by the hand of man. Some of the northern sector here is of partially chalky soil.

A father-to-son tradition prevails in the vineyards. Every year the *Foire aux Vins* takes place on the first Sunday in December, when growers and brokers can appraise the last vintage. There is also a Festival of Folk-lore.

The wine of Cornas, inclined to be rough at first, requires a few years to tone down to a velvety smoothness. It has a fine raspberry-like bouquet, plus a wealth of tannin and mineral salts which result in its being prescribed sometimes by the local doctors for many ailments. No doubt, like most good red wine used sensibly, it is a good tonic. Cornas is fairly long-lived, and experts accord a life of twenty years at least to the vintages of outstanding years.

Saint-Péray

Over the river from Valence is Saint-Péray, interesting for its production of the only real sparkling wine of the Côtes-du-Rhône, although some still white wines are also produced. Both types are based on the Roussanne and Marsanne vines.

More than a hundred years ago the growers of Saint-Péray (a M. Faure in particular) started experiments in applying the Champagne method to their white wines—that is, they tried to produce a second fermentation in the bottle (see page 28). Their success and the subsequent improvements they made popularised the wine locally—so much so that growers outside the parish bought the still Saint-Péray wine and then applied the 'Champanisation' treatment to it themselves. This resulted in legislation that no Saint-Péray wine made sparkling outside the vineyard area can claim the name.

The ordinary white Saint-Péray is a fairly assertive wine, with a pleasant aroma. One of its admirers was the composer Richard Wagner, and there exists a letter from him, sent from Bayreuth on December 2nd 1877, ordering a hundred bottles of Saint-Péray. He was then composing *Parsifal*, and the growers like to think that the juice of their grapes contributed to that opera.

Sparkling Saint-Péray is a good fruity wine, somewhat heavier than other sparkling wines. It has a pleasant bouquet and is usually moderately dark in colour for a white wine.

The Southern Sector

The other wines of the southern sector of the Rhône are possibly less known for, more than in any other area of France, the growers here belong to vast co-operatives, which arrange to accept their annual crop of grapes and then, with all the latest scientific aids, make the wine and sell it, of course paying the farmer.

Rationalisation of viticulture has become the main feature of post-war southern France and the smallholder finds it more convenient to become a member of one of the co-operatives, whereby his work is confined to cultivation of the vine and the gathering of the crop. Then he no longer has the worry associated with vinification, keeping the wine and negotiating with potential buyers for a sale. The co-operative cellars are usually administered by a committee who appoint an acknowledged viniculturist as manager to supervise the daily cellar routine.

The wines in the southern Rhône are mainly red and rosé, although one or two fortified sweet wines, such as the Muscat de Beaumes-de-Venise and Rasteau are also very popular.

The wines from many co-operatives are generally no more than '*vins de Café*' which are drunk very young, being distributed to the various large cities of France in tankers. However, many co-operatives produce excellent wines which they often bottle and market themselves, both for home consumption and for export.

A new development in co-operative marketing began in 1967, when eight co-operatives founded an organisation (the Cellier des Dauphins) as a central bottling cellar; this now markets over one million cases per year. Now dealing with the production of nine wineries, only the best wines are blended and bottled.

Clairette de Die

To the south-east of Valence, in the Drôme Valley, are the vineyards of Die. These produce a sparkling wine with a fine

Muscat flavour, made by the *méthode champenoise*, as well as some lesser-known still whites.

The Clairette de Die produced in the Drôme Valley is one of the oldest wines on record. It is mentioned by Pliny the Elder in his *Natural History* in A.D. 77: referring to Greek and Roman wines which, he says, are "sophisticated by adding honey, must of cooked grapes, resin or various berries", he writes that only one is excellent, called Aiglencos. It is described as a natural sweet wine, which remains sparkling, grown near Vocones—a district whose capital was Dea Augusta, the ancient city of Die.

Through the centuries the wines of Die have been protected: as long ago as A.D. 1380 a by-law forbade the bringing in to Die of any wine and grapes coming from territories outside; any that were detected were confiscated.

In 1910, Die was mentioned in one of the first classifications made by the I.N.A.O. (*Institut National des Appellations d'Origine Contrôlée*). In 1942 it was given *Appellation Contrôlée* status. On May 25th 1971, a new decree detailed the method of production, in particular defining the Die procedure of making sparkling wines excluding conserving agents.

Three types of wine are produced which can be called Clairette de Die. First, there is the Die method for sparkling wine. This produces a deliciously effervescent Muscat wine, made from a mixture of Muscat grapes (which give it a distinctive 'grapey' smell) and Clairette (which provides finesse). Second, the same wine without any Muscat grapes is called *Blanc de Blancs 'Brut'*; it is made from 100 per cent Clairette grapes. Third, there is a still, dry white wine, also made only from Clairette, which has A.C. status.

The other wines of the area are the Châtillon-en-Diois, a V.D.Q.S. (*Vin Delimité de Qualité Superieure*) until 1975 when it obtained its full *Appellation Contrôlée*. The main production here is of red wines, with the Gamay grape prevailing, but rosé and white wines are also made. The latter are made almost entirely from the Aligoté and Chardonnay white grapes. The vines for producing the *Appellation Contrôlée* wines are grown in thirteen Haut-Diois villages, and many wines are made at the Cave Co-operative at Die.

Tricastin

Just south of Montélimar is a new wine-producing area, the Côteaux du Tricastin, which only received its A.C. in 1973. However, the culture of the vine in this area is traditional: as evidence, there is a temple of Bacchus dating from the Roman epoch. Vineyard records have survived from the eleventh century and were maintained until the destruction of the vineyards by *phylloxera* (see page 16) in the nineteenth century.

The vineyards were rehabilitated and, in 1964, when their V.D.Q.S. status was acquired, they amounted to 365 hectares. Both the vineyard conditions and methods of production were of such a high standard that an application for the A.C. was made in 1972 and granted in July 1973. The vineyards had increased in size to 1,350 hectares by 1975, mostly by reclaiming soil that was previously heavily forested and stony.

Tricastin covers an area 20 by 15 kilometres, east of the line from Montélimar to Bollène on the left bank of the Rhône, and the *appellation* covers twenty Drôme and two Vaucluse communes. In the northern part, towards the chain of hills and south of the Bridge of Donzère, the soil is of ancient alluvial deposits. The centre region is a chain of hills, averaging 400 metres in height, with mixed soils—chalk, white sand and sandstone. In the south-east, the soils are mainly clay-chalk, very stony and dry, often with steep slopes. The western section on the edge of the plain of the Rhône is terraced; it is stony and chalky, the result of very old river deposits.

At Les Granges Gontardes there is something of more than mere local interest to the wine lover. This is Pierre Labeye's autovinification unit. This device, the autovinificator, is one of the most important contemporary innovations in the production of wine in hot vineyards. Essentially, the rising temperature in the fermentation vat acts on a valve which, when open, circulates the must at frequent intervals. This circulation keeps the temperature constant, instead of letting it rise too high and thereby endangering the whole process, and the mass of pulp is continually mixed. The advantage of the autovinificator is that it controls both the speed and quality of the fermentation. Its use has been successful in producing some of the finest wines of the area.

The style of wine which is being produced here is typically Rhône, and traditional vine varieties are grown. These are often staked to avoid damage from the violent Mistral blowing strongly down the valley. The red wines are made from Grenache (40 per cent), Cinsaut (20 per cent), Syrah (25 per cent), Mourvèdre (6 per cent), Carignan (7 per cent) and Picpoul Noir (2 per cent), with a limitation that no more than 20 per cent of the grapes used can be white varieties in the production of red wines. The best wines are superb, characteristically rich and red, of the Côtes-du-Rhône Villages style; the majority, however, are still sold in bulk for distribution throughout France.

Although white wines are legally permitted to be made, they are rarely produced. Five vine varieties are grown, of which the Grenache and Clairette are the most important.

Most of the wines produced in the region across the Rhône from Tricastin are very basic everyday light fruity wines, as might be expected from the grape varieties planted—Grenache, Cinsaut, Syrah, Carignan and other Côtes-du-Rhône *cépages*. The best wines of this Ardèche département are those of the Côtes du Vivarais, both red and white, with V.D.Q.S. status. However, as yet they are rarely found outside their production area.

Chusclan

Chusclan is the first of the trio of fine rosé wines produced on the west bank of the Rhône. The wines under this name come from five communes or parishes and are nearly all rosé. They are less fine than Tavel, but nevertheless have a fruitiness and bright colour that makes them very popular.

According to local usage, the vinification method is to leave the skins in contact with the must for only 10 to 12 hours. The wines may not be sold until six months after the vintage and each must be approved for quality by a commission of the I.N.A.O.

Vineyards in the area are thought to have been planted by the Romans. Certainly the wines were known in Europe in the eighteenth century and were often preferred to Tavel and Lirac.

In 1953, Chusclan was allowed to use its name for the Côtes-du-Rhône A.C. wines and now, of course, its wines are entitled to the *appellation* Côtes-du-Rhône Villages.

Laudun

Laudun's fine wines have been acknowledged from ancient times. The vineyards are the oldest in the Gard region and extend through three communes—Laudun, St. Victor-la-Coste and Tresques. Red, rosé and white wines are made, the latter often showing great finesse. Many vine varieties are permitted, principally the Clairette and Grenache, but also the Syrah, Cinsaut and Mouvèdre for the red wines, and several others for the whites (Ugni blanc, Bourboulenc, Picpoul, Calitor, Picardan, Roussette and Marsanne). The minimum alcoholic strength is 12 per cent for the white wines but 12.5 per cent for red and rosé. The Laudun *appellation* changes are the same as those for Chusclan.

Lirac

Lirac, a close neighbour of Laudun, makes rosé wine as well as red, plus a white which is little known outside the locality although it does occasionally feature on U.K. wine lists. The village is small but it has a flourishing wine co-operative. However, this does not mean that all the locals have plots of vines, for many growers are outsiders who own vineyards as a sideline; they are glad to share with the villagers the bounty of this elevated terrace site (which, paradoxically, is known as 'the plain'). The holdings are small, each averaging less than a hectare, so it naturally follows that most wine-making is a communal effort. The Comte de Ségriès is the owner of the most important vineyards, and he makes an interesting if somewhat light red wine, as well as rosé. Only a little white wine is made. The Lirac *appellation* is also shared by St. Laurent-des-Arbres, St. Genies-de-Comolas and Roquemaure.

Lirac is an excellent example of how vines have to suit the nature of the soil; they are selectively planted, according to the grower's experience, in the main soil types: stony ground, red gravel, sand and chalk—all similar to Tavel. Thus the 'blending' of the vines in the soil may be just as important as the blending of the grapes in the vats: another instance of the skill and care required to give balance, bouquet, fragrance and strength to the finished wine.

Tavel

Just to the south of Lirac is Tavel, where the vineyards produce probably the best dry rosé wine of France. The village of 1100 inhabitants has 900 hectares of vineyard and about 170 growers.

Tavel is perched on a steepish slope, among cypress wind-breaks and undulating olive groves. Whereas in some parts of the Rhône Valley vines are giving way to other crops, the reverse is true here and in the last few years many acres of former woodland have been added to the land already under vines. These extensions enable Tavel to satisfy the increasing demand for it from all over the world.

Although Tavel wine did not attain the dignity of its own name until the seventeenth century, it had a reputation before then. At that time the Port of Roquemaure, only a few miles from Tavel and on the opposite bank of the Rhône from Châteauneuf-du-Pape, was extremely busy; it is recorded that in one year as many as 12,000 casks of wine were loaded. Philip le Bel is credited with the saying: 'There is no good wine except Tavel', and its admirers included Louis XIV, the writers Balzac and Daudet, Brillat-Savarin, the celebrated gastronome, as well as members of the Papal Court at Avignon in earlier times. One may reasonably assume that it was also popular with the medieval troubadours. There is no doubt that in the eighteenth and nineteenth centuries the surrounding communes of Roquemaure, Lirac and Chusclan added their wines to those of Tavel, but now they have their own standing.

It was therefore probably no hardship for the inhabitants when, in olden days, no other wine or grapes were allowed into Tavel and they had to drink their own or go without. This ordinance was laid down apparently at a time when the wines had lost some of their earlier quality, and the growers were striving to improve matters. Old records tell something of this struggle and of the strict rules that were laid down: the village elders fixed the date of the harvest (this is still so in many parts of the wine growing world) and no one dared pick a grape until the town crier had announced when the vintage would begin. It was a matter of civic pride to abide by the regulation, which of course ensured that only ripe grapes were gathered, and few incurred the fine imposed for any breach of the rules. But in what was virtually a race with the vintage, not all men started equal: the seigneur of Tavel was given a three-day start!

Tavel rosé today is made by a judicious blending of several varieties of white and black grapes that are grown on three types of soil—stony, red and sandy. The lightly pressed berries are left for only one night in the vat before the skins are removed from the juice; this is sufficient to give the wine that brilliant pink colour which is such a delight to the eye. Tavel is drunk young and chilled and it goes well with almost any food; it is dry, full-bodied, with a generous bouquet and full of flavour. Its pinkness should not give anyone the idea that it is just a pretty wine for the ladies, for a good Tavel is usually 12 to 13 Gay Lussac (percentages of alcohol by volume)—by no means a trivial wine!

Much of the wine is produced on a co-operative basis (although several growers do 'domaine bottle'), and it is shipped to many countries in all continents—especially to North America. In bygone times Tavel had a reputation for travel, for it is said that many producers used to send a few barrels to be used as ballast on ships making the return trip to the West Indies. This was supposed to improve the wine greatly, just as brown sherries were said to benefit by a voyage to and from the east.

Châteauneuf-du-Pape

Across the river from Tavel is one of the greatest wine-producing areas of France. Strong like the sunshine that brings them to life, the red, vigorous wines of Châteauneuf-du-Pape have attained a well-deserved reputation throughout the world. The name, evocative of the wines' papal associations, is an unquestionable asset, but the wines stand on their own merit. They have a notable place in French vinicultural history, for they were the first to have regulations controlling their production and guaranteeing exact place of origin, thus establishing a tradition that all other important French wine districts have followed. (They also have the highest official *minimum* alcoholic strength—12.5 per cent.)

The first mention of Châteauneuf wine was in 1360. Innocent VI drank white wine from the region and in 1361 red wine from his own papal cellars. Documents of vinicultural interest date from the eighteenth century, one of particular note being a

The Grenache vine growing in the stony soil of Châteauneuf-du-Pape

letter from the Archbishop of Avignon to the 'Consuls' at Châteauneuf, warning them to beware of allowing early picked grapes into their cellars. Furthermore, the de Tulle family archives show that wines from their estate, Domaine de la Nerthe, known as '*Vin des Papes*', were becoming increasingly popular. By 1778 these wines were known in England and North America. Similar material, establishing the wines' pedigree, is in the hands of M. Lançon, one of the leading growers: these were issued in 1768 at Aix and they forbid hunting in the vineyards from 1st April until after the vintage. The expansion in the wine trade was paralleled by the local population—from 500 in 1700 to 1,000 in 1820 and 1,450 in 1850. The increase has not continued, however, and Châteauneuf, like other country villages, suffers from the migration of its inhabitants to the towns and cities.

Documentation in the nineteenth century is more plentiful; a 'Statistical Memorandum on the Département of Vaucluse' in 1808 mentions Châteauneuf as "a warm wine which is nevertheless delicate with finesse and which should be drunk in four years". Its vineyard at that time was forty hectares.

Jullien's book *The Topography of All Known Vineyards* (1822) places Châteauneuf-Calcernier in the first class and it particularly mentions la Fortia, la Nerthe and others. By 1873 the Châteauneuf vineyards totalled 500 to 600 hectares, but they were ravaged by *phylloxera* (see page 16) shortly afterwards. Destruction of the vines was followed by indiscriminate planting of fruit trees so that the farmers might scratch a living from the local arid soil, but this experiment was not particularly successful. However, the local cherries are well worth trying. The vineyards' recovery, led by men such as Commandant Duclos, ensured the continuation of the traditional great wines of Châteauneuf-du-Pape and the high reputation that they enjoy today.

Alphonse Daudet* called Châteauneuf-du-Pape the "King of Wines, Wine of Kings". No other southern wine can match its ruby colour, full bouquet, warm strength and delicacy on the

* French novelist and humorist (1840–1897)

palate, a combination that is based on the art of selecting and blending the juice of a choice of thirteen different grape varieties.

However, the full-bodied dry white wines with their fruit-cup bouquet should not be overlooked. They are produced in very small quantities and are a link with the wine formerly used for Mass at the papal palace. Just as the wines are linked across the ages, so too in unbroken tradition are the hardy workers today with their ancestors who cultivated the stone-covered red soil to produce a wine to grace the Pope's table.

The traditional proportions of grapes grown in the area have become less rigid and complicated with the planting of a 'new' vineyard area from reclaimed land. For red wines, planting has always been of Syrah, Grenache and Cinsaut; for white wines the Grenache blanc, Clairette and Bourboulenc are used.

On account of the *phylloxera*, mature vinestock had to be grafted on to roots resistant to the disease, which were mainly of American origin. Amongst the many varieties available, the following were chosen for this purpose as being most suitable for the soil and climatic conditions of this area, for it is not always realised that the basic stock or *porte-greffe* (the bearer of the graft) must be right for both the vineyard and the vines: Jacquez, Rupestris du Lot, Riparia Gloire de Montpellier, Solonis, Monticola and others. As new graftings are developed, certain of the older species (Muscadin, Picardin and Terret Noir) are tending to disappear, as they have low resistance to disease.

The many combinations of grapes permitted for red Châteauneuf-du-Pape account for the variations of flavour and quality in a range of wines that all bear the same name; each grower has his own particular style, which necessarily depends on the proportions of vines in his vineyards. No other wine-producing region of France shows such a large number of vine varieties (they were known to Abbé Rozie as early as the eighteenth century), and whereas the Pinot produces the great wines of Burgundy, the Syrah makes Hermitage and the Rousette St. Péray, it used to take no less than thirteen varieties to make the classic Châteauneuf-du-Pape. This is no longer necessary to accord with modern taste requirements, so nine varieties suffice for present-day production of, for example, Château Fortia.

White Châteauneuf-du-Pape is generally made solely from white grapes, the major varieties being Clairette and Grenache blanc. Of the two, the Clairette makes the sturdier wine, but the Grenache gives a finesse and volatility of fruity aromas that is not experienced with other wines of comparable alcoholic strength and body. The white wines account for less than 2 per cent of the total production. The method of cultivation for them is not particularly different from any other district, although mention should be made of the rapid wear on the plough-shares (and horse-shoes) of the stony soil, which were serious problems before the spread of mechanisation.

The vines planted have always been local growths and are intermixed in proportion in the vineyards. At harvest time the grapes are picked over by hand so that only the perfect examples are allowed into the Châteauneuf-du-Pape *cuvée*. The rest go to produce what is called *rapé*. The minimum quantity of *rapé* is 5 per cent of each picking. The exact amount is fixed annually by a committee, who consider the final condition of the grapes and also take into consideration any diseases of the vine which might have been prevalent in the region during the summer. In recent years a 15 per cent *rapé* was necessary on some estates.

Except for the Syrah grape, for which there are special regulations (see below), the vinestock is planted so that the shoots that will bear the grapes face north, because the Mistral in its constant blowing tends to turn the whole plant so that it faces south. The method of pruning varies only slightly within the regulations from estate to estate: i.e. a 'Short' pruning (two eyes and a replacement bud left) for all vines except the Syrah, which may have 'Long' pruning. The Syrah is the only vine allowed to be supported on wires. Other vines have to stand up for themselves.

Cairanne

Seventy five per cent of the present production at Cairanne is red wine, the remainder being divided between rosé and white. Although a handful of individual growers remain, most of them now belong to the co-operative, which has over 260 members. The wines are good with excellent bouquet, though perhaps too powerful for charm and elegance. In 1953 the excellent quality of its wines gave Cairanne the status of using its name with Côtes-du-Rhône, and eventually the *appellation* became Côtes-du-Rhône Villages (see page 61).

The newest of the two co-operatives in St. Cecile-les-Vignes has built overground vats, looking like three joined-up oil storage tanks, which contain concentric *cuves* or vats. These are not only space saving but also give excellent temperature control. The wines are traditional Côtes-du-Rhône—light, fruity and well balanced.

Almost due west are the vineyards of Rochegude, overlooked by the statue of Nôtre Dame de Puy. They produce red wine only from the Grenache, Carignan and a little Cinsaut. In the village of Suze-la-Rousse the co-operative cellars have a unique feature—huge cylindrical vats, which hold 48 *cuves*.

The nearby village of Bouchet produces mainly red wines (90 per cent), with the remainder rosé. The soil is sand and stone, and the grapes are the Grenache, Carignan, Cinsaut and Clairette. The growers use the nearby co-operatives at Suze-la-Rousse and Tulette, the latter having sufficient vineyards to require two co-opeative cellars. The dominant vines grown here are the Grenache and Clairette.

St. Maurice-sur-Eygues is an enchanting village; the vineyards, on stony or chalk soil, are mainly planted with the Grenache, but agriculture is also important here. The nearby twelfth century villages of Villedieu and Buisson produce 80 per cent red wines and 20 per cent rosé.

Visan is another charming village, typically Provençale. It is devoted solely to cultivation of the vine, the three varieties being the Grenache, Carignan and Clairette. Wines of good character are made from the various types of soil, and they are usually of high alcoholic strength. At Valréas the same grape varieties are grown, but they also cultivate other *cépages* which may only be used for *vins ordinaires*.

South along the winding D 46, one arrives at Vinsobres, Valréas, St. Pantaléon-les-Vignes and Rousset-les-Vignes (the latter being two small villages producing mainly red wines). These are the most northern vineyards of the meridional section of this region. They produce good characterful wines, the red being more supple than average. No doubt the climate, cooler than in vineyards a few miles further south, helps make a wine of lower alcoholic content that is therefore often pleasanter with a more pronounced bouquet. Although many grape varieties are grown, including the Grenache, Clairette, Cinsaut, Syrah and Mourvèdre, effort is now concentrated on the last two, as their cultivation is important for the production of quality wines.

Rasteau

About 30 kilometres to the south-west through vineyards brings the traveller to Rasteau which, apart from its red, rosé and golden white wines, also produces a most unusual one—a partly fortified white. For this only one vine is grown, the black Grenache, which draws from the pebbly marl of the soil a naturally golden wine. The skins are, of course, removed before they can tint the must in the vat. Then, during fermentation, a small amount of spirit is added to the wine. This stops the process of fermentation, preventing the complete transformation of the grape sugar into alcohol, as happens in the making of port, for example. The wine yeasts cannot continue to work once the spirit is added, so that there is a certain amount of natural grape sugar left in the finished wine. Thus the '*vin doux naturel*', which was first made in 1934, possesses both distinct sweetness and a high degree of alcohol. Only a few hectolitres are made annually. A *vin de liqueur*, according to regulations, may also be produced by the addition of alcohol to the unfermented grape juice. However, this drink, although pleasant, is not the same and not of the same quality (or price) as a *vin doux naturel*. The remaining Rasteau production is mainly a golden-yellow white wine, excellent as an apéritif.

Rasteau's local reputation is summed up in the ancient though chauvinistic claim that it possesses "the goodness of Pope Boniface, the wit of good King René, the simplicity of Saint Francis and the beauty of Queen Johanna". Even if the drinker cannot quite rate the wines so high, they are still well regarded, even when co-operative methods of production have replaced former traditional ways. The *appellation* decree for Rasteau establishes an unusual particular denomination—'*Rasteau Rancio*'—for wines which have obtained a peculiar taste (described as 'rancio') after a long period of maturation.

Rasteau wines have *Appellation Côtes du Rhône Villages* (granted in 1944), as do the wines from Sablet and Séguret, which are 95 per cent red and 5 per cent rosé made from the Grenache and Cinsaut.

Gigondas

The vines of Gigondas, producing red (70 per cent), rosé (20 per cent) and white wines (10 per cent) are grown on ideally exposed vineyards. The red wines are second only to Châteauneuf-du-Pape, with which they were combined in former times. Now they are, rightly, sold under their own name—and are often less expensive. At vintage time a proportion of the crop is discarded as *rapé*, the quantity of this being determined annually by a Commission.

In the main only the Grenache (90 per cent), Cinsaut and Clairette vines are grown on the chalky, stony soil of the high ground and on the stony soil in the plain.

In January 1971 Gigondas obtained its *Appellation Contrôlée* for red and rosé wines. The red wines are generous, with a fine bouquet; they are rich in flavour and usually high in alcohol. (14 to 15 per cent is normal, and even 17 per cent has been obtained!) They require a good many years both in cask and bottle to show off their finer characteristics.

Nearby Violès, essentially an agricultural village growing vegetables, tomatoes and melons, also produces mainly red wines from the Grenache (75 per cent) and Carignan (25 per cent) which flourish on the mainly stony soil. The wines adjacent to Roaix grow on heavy, partly stony soil, producing 75 per cent red wines and 25 per cent rosé from the Grenache, Cinsaut, Carignan and some Clairette. These two towns are covered by the *appellation* Côtes-du-Rhône Villages.

Vacqueyras

Vacqueyras produces almost solely red wine, although a very small quantity of white is made. Its *appellation* is Côtes-du-Rhône Villages. The vineyards abut on those of Gigondas and the wines are made from the same grape varieties—Grenache, Clairette and Cinsaut. Carignan is forbidden. Vacqueyras wines may not reach the Gigondas quality, but nevertheless they "Flatter the eye and palate of gourmets". And they are not trivial in style: I remember that, during the 1959 vintage, a notice board at the Vacqueyras Cave Co-operative proudly stated that a wine of over 18 per cent alcohol had been made!

Beaumes-de-Venise

The village of Beaumes-de-Venise is best known for its Muscat, which is a sweet dessert wine, frequently drunk chilled as an apéritif. The local co-operative also produces a good deal of red wine, which is marketed as Côtes-du-Rhône Villages, Côtes-du-Rhône and Côtes-du-Ventoux. *Vin doux naturel* and *Vin de liqueur* (see page 56) may also be made.

For the *vins doux naturel* the Muscat grapes, picked from only seven hectares of vineyards, are aged in cask, where they acquire a beautiful golden colour to add to their fragrance, strength and sweetness. They are, however, best drunk when fairly young, because the intensity of the bouquet diminishes with age. Some of the vines contributing to this wine are more than a hundred years old, grown on infertile sandy soil. Formerly they were cultivated on the supporting walls of the terraces, where the grapes were left to become dried—almost like raisins—before being gathered. These old vines have now been supplemented by others cultivated in the normal manner, but all contribute to the luscious character of the wine.

Production of the VDN (*vin doux naturel*) Muscat requires

a great deal of experience. The small Muscat grapes, all of which must be fully ripe, are pressed and fermented as for white wine; the fermentation is stopped by the addition of alcohol (this process is known as *mutage*) until a strength of 21 or 21.5 per cent is reached.

Côtes du Ventoux

The cultivation of the vine in the region of Côtes du Ventoux has continued and improved for a considerable time. In 1973, *Appellation Contrôlée* was granted for the best vineyards of the area, which lie east of a north-south line reaching from Vaison-la-Romaine through Carpentras to L'Isle de Sorgue, in the shadow of the Ventoux range of mountains.

The vines grow between 200 and 400 metres above sea level, on dry and calcareous soils. Over 10,000 hectares are under vine in 52 communes, worked by more than 4,000 growers. The main varieties grown are Grenache, Carignan, Cinsaut and Syrah, producing red, white and rosé wines. These tend to be lighter than the wines produced under the *appellation* Côtes-du-Rhône but, nevertheless, they are fruity and full of flavour. The area also is renowned for its production of superb table grapes, in particular the Muscat.

4

The Wine in Bottle

In choosing wines it is important to have some background knowledge of the A.C. laws and how they operate, what labels and bottle shapes can tell you about the wine, and which are the important vintages to look out for.

Throughout this book you will see references to A.C. and V.D.Q.S. wines—A.C. stands for *Appellation Contrôlée* (explained in detail below), and V.D.Q.S. for *Vin Delimité de Qualité Superieure*. V.D.Q.S. is a special *appellation* which is arranged for local wines rather than those fine wines which are covered by A.C., and most of these growths come from the south of the Rhône region. The controls imposed on them are similar to the A.C. regulations.

Appellation d'Origine Contrôlée

The Decrees for *Appellation Contrôlée* usually stipulate strict regulations for the culture of vines and the area to be cultivated (see Appendix 4 for details), including:

1. The actual defined area of plantation.
2. The vine varieties permitted (the *cépages*).
3. Minimum sugar concentration in the must.
4. Permitted production—hectolitres of wine per hectare (this is the *rendement*).

An upper excess production limit is also given (called the *plafond limité de classement*), and if the total crop goes above this it is declassified to a lower *appellation*.

5. The types of pruning that are permitted.

6. Condition of grapes and their production in accordance with local vinological practice.
7. Details of permitted irrigation which, where it is permitted, may be carried out by spraying and then not more than twice during a drought year and always before August 1st.
8. The methods of vinification.

The grower, however, is not subject to regulations regarding the compactness of his vines (planning of reconstructed vineyards depends upon the degree of mechanisation, as tractors require a greater space between the rows than horses), nor of the number of fruit-bearing branches on each vine, but he must keep the volume of his produce within the total limits of hectolitres per hectare*, as decreed by law.

Côtes-du-Rhône

All wines made in the Rhône Valley from permitted varieties within the rules of the *appellation* have the right to the controlled name 'Côtes-du-Rhône'. Many wines are entitled to their own individual *appellation*, such as Condrieu, Tavel, etc., and many of the superior growths come under the stricter regulation of 'Côtes-du-Rhône Villages'. There are, of course, very many different qualities of 'Côtes-du-Rhône' wines, depending not only on the vineyard site but also on the grape variety and the skill of the vintner.

The first declassification of "superior" wines is always to 'Côtes-du-Rhône'. This would happen, for instance, if the production had exceeded the permitted level, but the entitlement of the name is still dependent upon the production adhering to the 'Côtes-du-Rhône' *appellation* regulations.

Côtes-Du-Rhône Villages

A decree of the 25th August, 1967, defined the new name 'Côtes-du-Rhône Villages'. It had long been known that certain areas in the Rhône region, such as Châteauneuf-du-Pape, Tavel, Hermitage and Côte Rôtie, had established a hierarchy which

* 1 hectare = 2.47 acres; 1 hectolitre = 22 gallons = 11 dozen bottles

had gained universal recognition of quality production and quality control throughout the Côtes-du-Rhône region. Since World War II, special efforts have been made by many of the smaller parishes to attain a similar reputation, and since 1953 many of them have obtained the right to feature their village name on the label following the words 'Appellation Côtes-du-Rhône Contrôlée'.

The parishes (or '*villages*') which were given this recognition had undertaken to adhere to strict controls as regards the yield from the vineyards (35 hectolitres per hectare) and the establishment of higher minimum alcoholic strength than previously (12.5 per cent). They also accepted obligatory tasting for quality control.

In 1953 Gigondas, Cairanne, Chusclan and Laudun benefited from these new measures; in 1955 Vacqueyras was included, followed in 1957 by Vinsobres. In the 1960s another ten parishes applied for inclusion, and these have now been added to the list, giving a total of sixteen. These sixteen parishes have, by definition, set themselves the task of establishing quality. They have set a superb example which can only assist in increasing the renown of the whole of the Côtes-du-Rhône region.

It was obvious from a commercial point of view that the administrative requirements brought about by sixteen different place names, each with a relatively small production, would be complicated. The late Baron le Roy, who was President of the Vignerons, found a formula which solved this special problem. The regulations controlling production in these sixteen parishes are identical; there is a very strong family resemblance between them, particularly as the vine varieties used are similar and the variations in vineyard soils are minimal, so there was an obvious argument for allowing similar wines from two or more of these selected parishes to be blended together but to benefit from their particular name. Thus the definition Côtes-du-Rhône Villages was created.

The sixteen parishes concerned are:

Drôme: Rochegude, Rousset, Saint-Maurice-Sur-Eygues, Saint Pantaléon-les-Vignes, Vinsobres.

Vaucluse: Cairanne, Rasteau, Roaix, Sablet, Seguret, Vacqueyras, Valréas, Visan.
Gard: Chusclan, Laudun, Saint-Gervais.

Châteauneuf-du-Pape

Appellation Châteauneuf-du-Pape spreads from Châteauneuf-du-Pape commune across the border of four communes—Orange in the North, Courthézon in the East, Bédarrides in the South-East, and Sorgues in the South. Châteauneuf-du-Pape village, which is in the South-West, dominates its sector, of which it is the highest point, although not the highest point of the whole area.

The *appellation* area bounds in small plateaux and rising slopes to the hills so that a varied soil structure can be expected which, coupled with directional planting and many vine varieties, gives many different qualities to the final product. The stony soils are mainly on the plain, whereas the valleys and slopes are '*terre rouge*' and sand. The vines grown on stony soil generally produce wine of high alcoholic content which must be balanced by blending with less alcoholic wines from other soils, and this is the great secret of the vignerons' art, the subtle linking of various *cépages* to give a perfect final product.

It was not until after the end of World War I that efforts were begun to ensure the quality of the wine made in Châteauneuf. At that time viniculture was in a state of chaos: many of the wines were sold to other wine producing districts to bolster their production; foreign wines were introduced and hybrid grapes, which yield greater quantities of wine per vine than the 'pure strains', were indiscriminately planted.

The Syndicate at Châteauneuf

A group of vignerons set out to improve local conditions under the leadership of Baron le Roy, but they had to first agree that they would all keep to the newly devised and rigorous regulations.

Cellar in Châteauneuf-du-Pape

The original ideas proposed were:–

1. The delimitation of the area of production, based on the nature of the soil and its usage, as indicated by the growth of lavender and thyme. (When these two plants flourish together it is an excellent indication that the soil is also suitable for viniculture.)
2. The varieties of grapes allowed (all of noble origin) to be limited.
3. The method of culture (training and pruning) to be regulated.
4. The minimum alcoholic strength to be 12.5 per cent (Gay Lussac, percentage by volume).
5. A *triage* (separation of grapes according to quality) at the time of the vintage to be introduced, so that a minimum of 5 per cent are excluded from the *appellation*.
6. Production of *vin rosé* forbidden, and any unsound wines to lose their *appellation*.

The syndicate at Châteauneuf-du-Pape, which demanded and

obtained acceptance of these regulations for wine production from the Tribunals, was the precursor of the *Appellation Contrôlée*, but their principles were not accepted in law until May 1936.

The strict controls to which the growers agreed ensured that a high place of honour amongst the finest wines of the world was reserved for Châteauneuf-du-Pape. Many growers pride themselves in producing some of the very finest wines of the Rhône valley. A very large proportion of the crop is 'Domaine bottled', and its high quality is appreciated by connoisseurs all over the world.

Reflets de Châteauneuf-du-Pape

'Reflets de Châteauneuf-du-Pape' is a union of proprietors of leading estates which was founded in 1954. In contrast to the local co-operative, whose '*vins de café*' usually lack distinction, the 'Reflets' at Châteauneuf-du-Pape stand by the strictest rules and regulations of the *appellation*.

They market only the very finest wines under their distinguished seal '*Mise en bouteille aux Reflets*', each bottle being numbered and guaranteed. Endless trouble is taken over the vinification of their wines to ensure that outstanding quality is obtained. The partners vinify and treat their wines in their own cellars. They then have the choice of bottling all of them in their cellars, or of having the best of their *cuvées* bottled in the Reflets cellars—only the latter are entitled to the Reflets label.

The *vignerons* place their product (usually only the *têtes de cuvée*—very finest wines) before a committee composed of fellow members and an outside judge, usually an official of the *Institut National Appellation d'Origine Contrôlée*. They taste the wines without the grower's label and judge its quality, using an elaborate marking scheme. The wines must reach a high standard based on colour, bouquet, acidity and, most important of all, balance. In case of doubt the judge has a casting vote—a course of action rarely, if ever, taken.

The selected wines are bottled with all the care in the world and are binned in the Reflets cellar, each member having his own separate bins. Conditions in the cellars are perfect—on dry sandy soil and concrete pillars, with bins kept at the best temperature for gentle and smooth maturing. Usually the cellar holds 100,000 bottles, the red wines being a minimum of two years old and the whites, one year.

The members of the Reflets are subdivided into two sections: those with single estates and those who own many small sections of widely distributed vineyards, with a central cellar in the village. The latter suffer from the extra work entailed by their subdivided lands, yet they may benefit when bad weather strikes—especially when hailstorms occur in small areas. Labour and transport costs are naturally higher, but separation is a safeguard against spring frosts and summer hail, neither of which is necessarily widespread over the whole area.

A complete range of the wines of the 'Reflets' is available for tasting at their cellars in the village. The author's firm represents this union in the U.K.

The major blends for the classical red wine of Châteauneuf-du-Pape are made up from four groups of grapes with the following major components. This list was compiled by Commandant Duclos (owner of Château de la Nerthe and one of the pioneers of more rigorous standards in the production of Châteauneuf wines) at the end of the last century.

Group I
Grenache, Cinsaut (20%) giving warmth, liqueur and mellowness

Group II
Mourvèdre, Syrah, Muscadin, Vaccarèse (30%) giving solidity, durability and colour with a pure refreshing flavour

Group III
Counoise, Picpoul (40%) giving vinosity, charm, freshness and bouquet

Group IV
Clairette, Bourboulenc (10%) white grapes giving fire and brilliance to the wine

A more modern scheme of replanting is with vines in the following proportions:

40–60% Grenache
30–10% Syrah
20% Cinsaut, Mourvèdre, Counoise, Vaccarèse
10% Clairette, Bourboulenc

It is amazing that this formula has stood the test of time and is still in use today.

The Local Professional Organisations

The suitably named Maison du Vin in Avignon's busy main street houses the most important organisations covering the many interests of Rhône Valley vintners. Each organisation has its own specific function and includes committees covering commercial interests (merchants), the Co-operatives, the V.D.Q.S. producers, wholesalers and retailers, all of whom are represented on the *Comité Interprofessionnel des Vins des Côtes-du-Rhône*.

The C.I.V.C.D.R. was created in 1955 to promote Rhône wines and co-ordinate the efforts of Rhône producers and merchants, and the committee also includes brokers, hoteliers, tourist advisors and representatives of the I.N.A.O. It also serves as technical advisor (it has its own laboratory and tasting room facilities), collates statistics and promotes the importance of the Rhône with its publications and public relations efforts throughout the world. The director, Pièrre Ligier, is a mine of the most useful information and visitors are always welcome at their offices in 41 Cours Jean Jaurès.

Rhône Vintages

It is very difficult to be dogmatic about Rhône vintages. The valley is blessed with abundant sunshine, so the majority of harvests are good or very good. Therefore much depends upon the skill of the maker. The two sectors of the area can be expected to show variations, because they each have their own microclimate, but an overall picture indicates an average of what can be expected:

	North		South	
	Red	White	Red	Rosé
1978	7	7	7	7
1977	5	6	5	5
1976	6	6	6	6
1975	4	6	3	4
1974	4	6	5	5
1973	6	5	4	7
1972	6	5	5	5
1971	7	7	6	7

7=Best, 6=Very good, 5=Good, 4=Medium,
3=Below average (Scale 1—7)

Before buying in quantity, I always recommend tasting a selection of different wines so as to make certain that you are getting the best value for your own palate. Variations in style from a single region can be enormous, particularly in the southern Rhône where the choice of vine combinations is large. Finally, I have one specific recommendation: always buy a wine you can afford—you will not completely enjoy any wine which is beyond your means.

Labels, Bottles and Serving Rhône Wines

The introduction of E.E.C. regulations has meant uniform labelling throughout the Common Market. The labels, therefore, give all the basic information required. They state:

The exact name of the wine with its full *appellation.*
The name of the bottler and his address.
The average contents of the bottle.
The country of origin (i.e. France).

Eventually, all quality wines (A.O.C. and V.D.Q.S.) will be tasted to ensure a basic minimum standard; in fact, this type of tasting is mandatory now for V.D.Q.S. wines. Extra information is allowed on the label, including the vintage year of production, details of the colour of the wine, the main vine varieties used, the history of production and so on, but these must be described in such a way as to avoid any possible confusion with the mandatory information. For example, there must be no implication of a wine coming from an individual estate unless it actually does.

Various bottle shapes are used for Rhône wines but the majority are bottled in the standard Burgundy shape; for Châteauneuf-du-Pape wines this is embossed with the Papal coat of arms on the bottle's shoulder. The Normande shape—a slightly long-necked Bordeaux or claret-type bottle—is often used in the southern region. The flûte (the elongated German shape associated with many white wines) is used by Château Grillet and some bottlers of rosé wine.

All Rhône red wines benefit from decanting—a process which airs the wine and allows the bouquet to develop after its long sojourn in bottle—even young wines. They should always be served at room temperature. Rhône white wines are best served chilled, but they should never be too cold as their lovely fruity bouquet would be masked. In my opinion these wines have much more flavour than the whites from Burgundy and can therefore be matched with strongly flavoured food. I normally prefer sparkling St. Péray as an apéritif, and Clairette de Die as an accompaniment for desserts and ripe fruit.

The enjoyment of Rhône wines is enhanced by food. The wines tend to be big, full and rich, often with high alcoholic strength, and the red wines, in particular, need food to really show their paces. The traditional combination of 'red meat with red wine', 'white meat and fish with white wine' and 'sparkling dry wine with anything' are useful guidelines, but it is worth going further and matching lighter food with lighter wines and only serving the heavier wines with the richest food. For more details see page 103.

What Rhône Wines Taste Like

A tour of the Rhône vineyards, whether physically or through these pages, will indicate the many soil varieties of the area, the many vine varieties grown and the different methods of vinification. The quality of the wines also varies with the size of the crop—the larger the production the less concentrated are the flavours in the wine. To these variables we can add the difference in maturing—whether it takes place in small or large wooden casks or in stainless steel vats, possibly protected from the air by a covering of nitrogen—a neutral gas.

The most fascinating aspect of the Rhône wines, in contrast to those from other areas of France, is that many of the finest red wines use white grapes in their making—this is to temper the fire of some of the red varieties such as the Syrah. How much softer St. Joseph is than Cornas, the latter wine made only from the Syrah.

Notwithstanding the abundance of sunshine, not all Rhône wines are high in alcohol: Côte Rôtie, for instance, has a permitted lower level of 10 per cent, but in the southern sector red wines of up to 15.5 per cent are not unknown. Personally I find that the best balanced wines average 12½ to 14 per cent alcohol—higher than this certainly means a harder and much less elegant wine.

The White Wines

The Rhône white wines are always dry with plenty of body. The northern sector varieties—made from the Viognier, Marsanne and Roussanne—are always well balanced, with a good, full flavour. Although they do not have a marked acidity, as do some of the Mâconnais or white Burgundies, they nevertheless age extremely well and can live for decades, ageing gracefully and smoothly, darkening in colour, never losing the full flavour that characterised their youth.

White wines from the southern sector use a more varied collection of vines; although they have the same dryness as the northern whites, they tend to have a fruity bouquet which is to me often reminiscent of German wines and totally uncharacteristic of the dry wines of eastern France. The ordinary Côtes-du-Rhône blancs are very pleasant in their youth, but it is the great Châteauneuf-du-Pape blancs that are the finest in the region. These full-bodied wines, in harmony with their fruity bouquet and flavour, are a delightful contrast to the more sedate, less obvious white Burgundies. I think they can more easily be enjoyed on their own, as apéritifs, as well as to accompany highly seasoned food.

The Pink Wines

The rosé wines of the Rhône are unique—dry but full-bodied, with an elegant bouquet. The balance, of course, is determined by the technique of the maker, who must time the period of contact between the skins and the juice so as to retain the essential qualities of a dry rosé and avoid producing a light red wine.

Tavel and Lirac are full-bodied rosés, but the lesser vineyards tend to produce much lighter wines, which are often more attractive for drinking on their own without food.

The Red Wines

How can the myriad red wines be described in a few words? The Côte Rôties with their raspberry flavour can still vary enormously, depending on the soil which bred them and the cask that matured them. They have a tendency to be harsh in their youth, but they flower into magnificence and the best need time in cask and bottle to show their best. The amount of Viognier in the blend of these wines is small, so that the Syrah fire is not too well tempered. By contrast, Hermitage and Crozes Hermitage are rounder and smoother earlier in their life, due to the addition of the Marsanne and Roussanne to the Syrah. Long, slow ageing of these wines is essential, and many experts have placed the best on a par with certain Côte d'Or wines. St. Joseph wines are similar but they have less depth, as would be expected from the less well situated vineyards on the west bank of the Rhône.

The red wines from the southern sector vineyards vary enormously in flavour. I divide them into three categories: the Beaujolais type (made by *macération carbonique*), which has a fruity bouquet and a light flavour; the Burgundy type, deep-toned with a full bouquet and smooth body, made from a well-chosen mixture of grape varieties; and the claret type—dry, tannic wines with less finesse, using fewer white grape varieties and made from the Syrah and Grenache. This results in a fine wine that is high in alcohol.

The Côtes-du-Rhône and 'Villages' reds tend to be made in the first two styles and are ready for drinking when they are young, even in their first year, when they possess body and a ripe soft fruity flavour. Vinification tends to be aimed at making them ready for early consumption and, in general, it is the individual *appellations* that are worth laying down for the future. These are the wines which can live for decades, losing their youthful fruit as they mature and changing into wines with a definite relationship to Burgundy—full, smooth and well-flavoured, but not too obvious.

Every wine has its own definite style, and many producers have sufficient stocks to mature their wine for several years in wood. The differences that may result from a long period in wood—giving ripeness and flavour—are bestowed by the individual producer making use of traditional methods of wine production as well as more recent knowledge about the behaviour of young wines. Therefore most of the finest wines are bottled after two years or longer.

5

Visiting the Region

Perhaps it is the combination of many factors—history, scenic splendours, wine and gastronomy—which makes the Rhône area so exciting and the ideal setting for a leisurely and fascinating wine lover's and gourmet's holiday. People who rush through the valley in a day or even two are missing a great deal.

How to Travel

It is easy enough to reach the area, either by the various express trains or, nowadays, by air to Marseille or Lyon. But, once there, the wine loving traveller unfortunately cannot rely on public transport for visiting the vineyards. Bus services are adequate between the main towns, but do not give opportunities for getting off the beaten track and for seeing cellars; as yet, there are not any planned tours taking in the vineyards of any regions. Therefore it is essential either to take your own car or to hire one, and then to allow at least several days for seeing something of the main vineyards and sampling local gastronomic specialities. Unless you are also intending to devote some time to seeing towns such as Châteauneuf, Avignon, Vaison-la-Romaine and Orange in detail, perhaps concentrating on works of art, then a period of about five days to a week will give a fair impression of the vineyards and not prove too taxing, although of course it will be necessary to move around, as it is not possible to see the whole of the valley from one stopping place.

When to Go

The best time of the year to go is virtually from May to September, although it should be remembered that, in August, it is not only very hot indeed, but accommodation will be very scarce: check on school and public holidays rather than risk being disappointed. The same advice applies to any region where one of the music or arts festivals are being held during the summer. (The French Government Tourist offices in various capital cities or any good travel agency will be able to inform you about this type of activity).

Maps

The Michelin Maps 73, 77 and 81 cover all the wine areas in detail and are likely to be more helpful to the explorer than any single general map. For anyone interested in the historical background and artistic treasures of the towns, the green guides by Michelin, *Vallée de la Rhône* and *Provence*, include maps and much additional detail, but they are only available in French, so some will need an English guide book.

Suggested Tours

To see the northern vineyards of the Rhône Valley, a start might be made either from Lyon or Vienne. The autoroute from Lyon to Vienne makes this a fairly quick but not particularly interesting journey. At Vienne, cross the river—both the autoroute and the N7 (formerly the main highway to the Riviera) continue on the east bank—and follow the more leisurely N86 to Condrieu. From here down to the twin towns of Tain and Tournon, which straddle the Rhône, there are vineyards alongside most of the road: Côte Rôtie (where the different colour of the soils of the Côte Blonde and Côte Brune are easy to pick out), Condrieu itself, the tiny estate of Château Grillet, tucked in a curve of the slopes that rise from the river and, finally, Tain l'Hermitage itself.

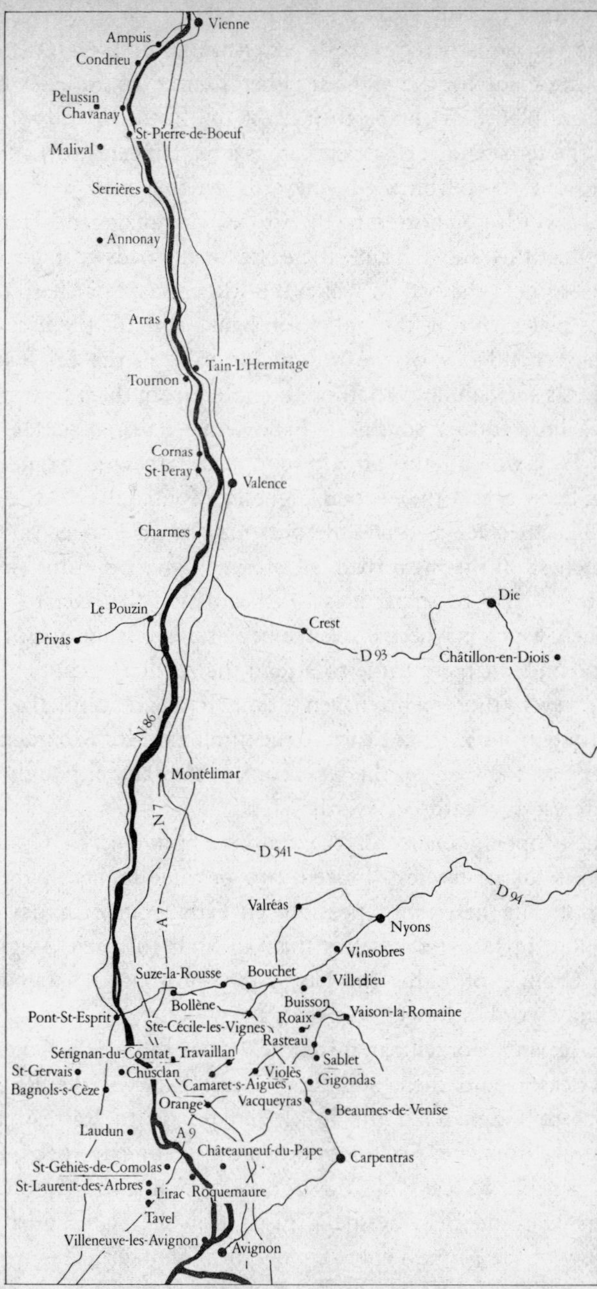

Touring map of the Rhône Valley showing towns and villages

The vineyards here are fairly extensive and therefore a stop might be made for the night at either Tain or Tournon—where there are plenty of things to interest the historian and where, from the terrace of the castle, there is a magnificent view across the Rhône to the terraced vineyards on the other side. It is equally worth going up into the Crozes Hermitage and Hermitage vineyards above Tain—there are small roads to take you there—to note the way in which the Rhône makes a sharp turn at this place, cutting through steep banks towards the east.

The second day of the tour might take in the St. Joseph vineyards surrounding Tournon, going on from there to Cornas and, a little further south, St. Péray. An excursion to Die on road D93 would take an afternoon, and then it would be possible to spend the second night in Montélimar. For those who like spectacular drives, detours may be made over various 'corniches' off the main road, all of which give beautiful views. If there is time to spare, it is worth crossing the river to visit Valence, which is where Provence begins; here, at the age of 16, Napoleon Bonaparte came to attend the Artillery School.

However, those who haven't time to spare can take the autoroute from Valence down to the turning off for Montélimar. Otherwise, the road on the west bank is pleasant, although not of interest as regards vineyards.

The stopping place for the third night might be Orange, which is full of interest. Indeed, two or three nights might be spent staying here, with possibly an extra couple of days at Avignon. In fact it takes less than an hour to reach Avignon from Orange, on either the N6 or the autoroute A7, but it is certainly worth a longer stay than a few hours.

On leaving Montélimar, by road D73, one can see the Côteaux du Tricastin and then, still on the east bank of the Rhône, detour to Grignan on the D541 and go on to Rasteau and Vaison-la-Romaine. On this route, using secondary roads, it is also possible to pass by Vinsobres and Cairanne, Gigondas, Vacqueyras and Beaumes-de-Venise, all in the plain under the shadow of the Mont Ventoux range of mountains. This would make quite a long day, but a rewarding one—though don't forget to leave time for a rest and, possibly, a siesta, if you are travelling in a season when the mid-day heat can be exhausting.

As Châteauneuf-du-Pape is virtually halfway between Orange and Avignon, on the D17, it is up to the individual to decide the point from which to visit this most important vineyard—but do leave sufficient time to see it in some detail and to visit more than one cellar if possible. The variations in soil are remarkable and, as the white wines of this region are little known in the U.K., this might be an opportunity to try some of them, as well as the famous reds.

The vineyards of Chusclan, Laudun, Lirac and Tavel, all on the west side of the Rhône, would make another separate day's excursion so as to get to know this area of the Gard. These vineyards in the southern plain are well signposted. A detour to the great aqueduct, the Pont du Gard, might also be included, taking the N100 from Avignon. However, if you are pressed for time it would be possible to visit this area in an afternoon: make a circuit from Orange and start by seeing Châteauneuf-du-Pape, then cross the river at Avignon, with its famous bridge, to see the western vineyards and return to Orange on the D976 or the autoroute A9.

If you would like to follow any other tours, the French Tourist Office will be able to recommend some particularly interesting routes. But on any planned tour, do leave time to enjoy the food, which is beautifully prepared in most of the local restaurants—even those which look rather humble from the outside. All will display price lists with their specially arranged menus, and remember that it is often far cheaper to eat a set meal—even of four courses—than it is to order one or two dishes à la carte.

Visiting Vineyards

Rhône wine makers are renowned for their hospitality and always welcome guests to taste their selection of wines. Most vintners have signs on their houses indicating their willingness to receive visitors: these often read '*Dégustation—ventes*'

('Tastings—wines for sale'), and appointments need not be made before visiting the smaller establishments. However, you should check in advance when the French public holidays fall, as the tasting rooms may be closed then (either the local Tourist Information Office or your hotel should be able to advise you about this). Nor should you try to visit any establishments during lunch time (12.00 noon to 2.00 p.m.) or after 6.30 p.m.

A visit of this kind does not mean that you have to buy any wine, although you would probably want to purchase a couple of bottles to enjoy later. Generally, the very well-organised tasting rooms, even those which are small, do not expect visitors to purchase as a matter of course. Nor is it necessary to tip—unless this is obviously expected by a guide—but occasionally a donation to the upkeep of the tasting room might be made.

If you want to visit a Rhône establishment for the purpose of seriously studying the wines, then most companies representing Rhône firms in the U.K. can arrange specific appointments with their principals. Your wine merchant may be able to fix this for you, unless you already know an importer. However, it really is essential to give at least six weeks' notice of a visit, so don't try to make any last-minute arrangements. Again, growers naturally appreciate a visitor buying a few bottles; prices always include all taxes and, if you are driving home, the bottles can provide good drinks for any picnics en route! Otherwise, you must have a bill to show the Customs for any wine you bring into the U.K.

For visitors to the Rhône who wish to taste the main *appellations*, a full list of growers and co-operatives which should be visited can be obtained from the C.I.V.C.D.R., Maison du Vin, 41 Cours Jean Jaurès, 84000 Avignon—you should ask for their booklet *Parcours du Vignoble*. You will find an abbreviated version of this publication, giving the most important names, at the back of this book in Appendix 6.

Visitors to the various wine fairs (see page 109) are normally expected to pay a small charge for the wines they taste. However, the quantities poured are generous and the opportunity of tasting a wide range of wines and, possibly, meeting many interesting people should not be missed.

The Rhône Route

Vienne is an ideal starting point for the historian. Particular points of interest are its Roman temple, which is only one of two of this type still existing on the soil of ancient Gaul; the stretch of Roman road which is maintained in the public gardens, and the Roman theatre, which seats no fewer than 13,000 people. None of these sights should be missed.

Historic religious buildings include the cloister of the Benedictine Abbey of St. André-le-Bas, dating from before 1150, and the Church of St. Pierre originating in the sixth century. A building which was a cathedral until its destruction by the Saracens in about A.D. 732 now houses a museum with a large collection of Roman remains, mosaics, pottery, sculpture and frescoes.

The wine tour itself starts when the Rhône is crossed at Vienne. Ampuis is reached after a few kilometres southwards on the N86, and this village is the beginning of the Côte Rôtie.

Condrieu

Immediately south of the Côte Rôtie is Condrieu which, like Côte Rôtie, has its vine roots deep in history. Ancient writings state that these vineyards were founded by a Helvetian tribe sent from the Swiss lowlands by their conqueror, Julius Caesar, after he had crushed the great Gallic revolt. This gives the wine a birth certificate of approximately 58 B.C. During the following century it is mentioned in Latin works, Martial remarking on the violet perfume which connoisseurs discern (possibly by suggestion) in the present-day wine. In the fourteenth century when the Papacy ruled from Avignon, itself a noble wine centre, the Popes regularly had Condrieu shipped down the Rhône for their Christmas festivities.

Most of the local wine is bought by the famous restaurants of Lyon and Vienne, so it is little known in Britain. The

American writer, Waverley Root, in *The Food of France* (Cassell, 1958), says Condrieu is the most seductive minor wine he knows and advises those who eat locally not to miss it. The Beau Rivage restaurant on the banks of the Rhône has an excellent cellar, ideal for studying many of the local wines.

Leaving Condrieu, it is worthwhile making a detour into the quiet countryside high above the Route Nationale. There are several delightful roads to the small town of Pelussin, the road from Chavanay being particularly beautiful, with road signs indicating that this is a circuit of the gorges around Mont Pilat. From Pelussin, with the aid of the Michelin map, several circuits can be made back to the main road, the N86, either directly or through Malival which is a lovely old village completely unspoiled by modernisation—except for the myriad T.V. aerials. The whole area, which is part of the Pilat natural regional park, has ideal picnic spots in the middle of countryside where, with a little imagination, you can turn the clock back several centuries. Continuing on the main road at St. Pierre de Boeuf, a sign invites you to '*Vivez heureux en Ardèche*', for you are now in that region.

A few kilometres further on at Serrières, the old church of St. Sornin, dating back to the fourteenth century, now houses the Rhône Mariners Museum. A detour from here on the N519 towards Annonay is worthwhile for the superb Rhône views as you travel up the hillsides; orchards and vines are interspersed with many picnic sites and the complete circuit includes Annonay, an attractive town in a valley surrounded by mountains built on two sides of a gorge, a mixture of very old and very new buildings.

Tournon

The last lap of the circuit on the RN82 is a picturesque descent back into the Rhône Valley with delightful views at every turn, vast orchards on the hillsides arranged so that from a distance they appear like giant vineyards. The continuing drive towards Tournon follows a road squeezed between the river on the left and orchards and vineyards on the right, overlooked by darkly-wooded hillsides.

From Tournon there are many beautiful tours through the various gorges and I would highly recommend a careful study of the Michelin map to anyone with an hour or two to spare, so that some of this spectacular scenery can be enjoyed.

Tournon itself is a pleasant town, less noisy than Tain on the opposite bank of the Rhône. Its castle has terraces with magnificent views, many fifteenth century houses have been preserved and there are some fine tapestries and frescoes in the Lycée des Garçons. Here too are several moderately priced hotels and restaurants.

Hermitage

Across the Rhône the great vine-clad hill of Hermitage rises to form a sunny amphitheatre of terraces high above the riverside town of Tain. The hill loses hardly a ray of any day's sunshine. A few small chalets dot its slopes but one scarcely sees a tree—nothing but the vines and the pattern of the retaining walls marching up the slopes like a gigantic ladder. Some sectors of vineyard proudly display the owner's name. This magnificent sight is often missed from the road, except for a possible fleeting reflection in a rear view mirror, so make a point of stopping. It is debatable whether the panorama is more magnificent at dawn or dusk, but it is best viewed from the west bank of the Rhône at Tournon.

The Hermitage vineyard takes its name from a celebrated but anonymous hermit, for no evidence exists as to exactly who he was. One story makes him a Christian refugee from the Romans, who fled to the mountainside where vines were sent down to him from heaven—vines that ripened in a single night and produced instant wine! Other stories relate that in the thirteenth century Blanche of Castile, Queen and regent of France, granted the land to the Chevalier Gaspard de Sterimberg when he returned badly wounded from the Crusades. There he became a hermit, cultivating his grapes and devoting his life to worship in the small chapel, dating from Gallo-Roman times, that crowns the hill. Novelist Alexandre Dumas, visiting Hermitage in 1834, states that the hermit was a poor man of the early seventeenth century. From all of this it can be seen that the place was determined to have a hermit—perhaps it had more than one!

The legend of Roman times is certainly feasible, for the hill appears to have been the scene of a victory by Fabius over the Arvernes, and those early champions of Rhône wines, Pliny and Plutarch, mention the Hermitage wine. If we accept Dumas' version, then his hermit may have been the grower who made the wine that King Louis XIV, *le Roi Soleil*, sent as a gift to King Charles II in 1666—the year of the Great Fire of London. Records show that around this time English noblemen, who had returned home again with the Stuart monarch after living abroad during Cromwell's Protectorate, were importing the occasional barrel of Hermitage wine.

The Sterimberg chapel overlooking the Hermitage vineyards

Cornas, St. Péray

A little way downstream, where the River Isère pours its glacial water from the Alps into the Rhône, is the little town of Cornas. Cheek by jowl with Cornas, on the opposite bank to Valence, overlooked by the ruins of Château de Crussol in a gorge at the foot of the Cévennes (readers of R.L. Stevenson's *Travels with a Donkey*, 1879, will remember these mountains), is Saint-Péray. The land is rich for producing fruits, but it is also of interest to the geologist, as many fossils have been found there. The view from the Château of the Rhône and the Drôme, which joins the Rhône nearby, is magnificent.

Leaving St. Péray, the road passes through beautiful villages, one of the most attractive being Charmes, which truly lives up to its name, until Le Pouzin is reached. From here, a short detour of ten miles through a narrow valley along the N104 leads to Privas. This is a typical French town with an agricultural museum, and it also proclaims itself as a capital of *marron glacé*, the delectable chestnut sweet.

From Pouzin the route goes east, crossing the Rhône and taking the inland N93 road towards Die; this is a very picturesque drive, straight towards the mountains with their craggy peaks, among farmland dotted with old houses. Following the N93, this road from Valence is the old route taken by Hannibal crossing the pre-Alp countryside; it continues to the town of Crest, which is dominated by its castle on the hillside. Here is the Clairette de Die country (see page 28). The road follows the valley and is dominated by the rugged mountains on the right and on the left by the vineyards, which are planted in irregular patterns amongst the farm houses. The drive continues from one beautiful valley to another and signs at the roadside invite travellers to taste (and of course buy) the local wines.

Continuing the journey on the N93, the route then joins the N539 towards Châtillon-en-Diois. Here there appear to be more orchards than vineyards, pruned low in exactly the same order as the vineyards. In fact, the orchards are planted on the plain near the roadside and the vines, where their cultivation is possible, are on the hillsides. In addition to vines and fruit, the area is renowned for its lavender: the bushes cluster in lines that, from a distance, resemble blue-grey mole-hills. Another local speciality is walnut oil, such a delight in salads—watch out for *huile de noix* on menus.

The route then returns to the Rhône Valley, the N538 from Crest to Montélimar being another enjoyable drive. Time should be allowed to stop, both for tasting and to sample the various types of nougat which are made in this centre of the French nougat industry. It has been a local speciality for centuries and Montélimar is the ideal area for its production, making use of the deliciously-flavoured local almonds and honey from both the Alps and Provence.

Tricastin

A few miles further south is a relatively recent addition to the Rhône wine map—Tricastin. Rather than become an extension of Côtes-du-Rhône or Villages, the growers decided to market their wines under their historic name. (This area is also famous for its black truffles—gourmets should note them on local menus.)

At the southern extreme of the area Bollène, which names itself 'Town of the Sun, Door of Provence', is better known for its impressive hydro-electric scheme 'Usine Blondel' than for its wines. It lies on the east bank of the Donzère Mondragon Canal, opposite Pont St. Esprit. Within a few miles of the town are the 'Collines de Barry', site both of a troglodyte village and a superb camping place for holiday-makers. Also to be seen are the Château-Fort of the thirteenth century and numerous chapels of the Middle Ages, one of which houses a museum. Agriculture is important and Bollène's fruit and vegetable market is renowned.

St. Gervais, Chusclan

The road continues, crossing the canals with their hydro-electric installation and then the Rhône, passing by the uranium refinery at Pont St. Esprit. Here it is worth stopping to look at the picturesque rugged area to the north-west and possibly to taste the delightful wines from the Côteaux de Vivarais, produced in the region directly across the Rhône from Tricastin. From Pont St. Esprit the route goes through Bagnols-sur-Cèze (from which a small 6 kilometre detour can be made to St. Gervais, which makes Côtes-du-Rhône Villages, both red and rosé), onto the plain, heading towards Chusclan. There are vineyards in all directions as far as the eye can see.

Nearby, for those who are scientifically-minded, is the French Atomic Centre of Marcoule, which can be seen from a pleasantly-situated viewing area on the hillside at Belvédère. The pavilion at this spot contains exhibits and material explaining the atomic processes, the safeguards for preventing disasters and it also gives details of the adjacent protective zone, where monitoring tests of animals and vegetation are regularly taken, so as to check the radiation levels.

The terrain near Laudun is of two quite different types: an elevated part, giving magnificent views over the Rhône Valley, and a plain (*'le camp de César'*), where Julius Caesar set up his camp to control the valley. The main concern of this historic area is wine, but other forms of agriculture also play important parts—cereals, feeding stuffs for animals, olive oil, sugar-beet and herbs are all cultivated.

Lirac, Roquemaure

Much of the land around the village of Lirac is given over to cereals and fruit and is typically Provençal—cypress trees, pines, slopes covered with vines and olive trees. Other places of interest are the three other villages that share Lirac's *appellation*—St. Laurent-des-Arbres, enclosed in the ramparts of its old fortifications; St. Genies-de-Comolas; and Roquemaure, on the banks of the Rhône where Hannibal's legions crossed the river on the historic march across the Alps into Italy.

Roquemaure (conveniently situated on the main Orange-Nîmes road) has a tasting cellar, where the whole range of Lirac wines can be sampled.

Tavel

The road to Tavel is surrounded by little hills and vineyards on high ground. Every possible square metre is cultivated with vines, with rows of cypress trees to break the force of the winds. The new autoroute and the modern buildings have transformed this formerly sleepy wine village into a thriving modern community.

From Tavel, passing through Roquemaure and across the new Rhône bridge, the finest and most important Rhône vineyard area is ahead: Châteauneuf-du-Pape. However, if the tourist has travelled by the more direct fast route from Valence, he will have seen the vineyards disappear and the changing landscape given over to farming and fruit growing. There are more olive groves; cypress trees stand as windbreaks against the seasonal battle with the Mistral and, in villages with Romanesque churches, hard-pruned plane trees spread a leafy parasol so as to give shade to the *boule* players in the square. The clear air, the brilliantly coloured countryside, the fantastic light all proclaim that one is in the heart of Provence.

Châteauneuf-du-Pape

Soon the traveller is in what is by far the most extensive wine region of the Rhône, with the eight square miles of Châteauneuf-du-Pape as the centrepiece.

Châteauneuf-du-Pape is an ideal centre from which to discover the vineyards of the southern Rhône. The two famous restaurants in the middle of the village overlook the vineyards, and they have excellent selections of many vintages of Châteauneuf-du-Pape to complement their fine cooking.

The village of Châteauneuf-du-Pape itself, equidistant from Orange and Avignon, sprawls down the gentle hillside that is dominated by the ruins of the Château above. The keep, which had remained almost intact with its vaulted rooms since it was first built in the twelfth century, was restored at the beginning of the century so as to allow visitors to view the panorama of the Rhône Valley. Unfortunately it suffered a final outrage in 1944 when the retreating Germans blew it up. The remaining façade has been buttressed and consolidated. The imposing ruins are still sufficient to show the dignity of the castle in its prime. The rebuilt cellars are a magnificent setting for the banquets which are regularly held there to proclaim the quality of Châteauneuf-du-Pape wines. Also worth visiting is the wine museum at Caves Père Anselme.

Deployed amongst the vineyards are the domaines or individual holdings with their red roofs, partly protected from the north wind by rows of cypresses and other trees. Gently undulating, with small rises in the ground and little plains, this compact viticultural area of Châteauneuf-du-Pape contains many varied soils, resulting in a variety of fine, perfumed, full-bodied wines.

Alternatively, you could base yourself at Orange, an ideal centre from which to explore this part of the region.

Orange

Formerly a Roman colony, Orange has retained some of the most fascinating classical remains in Provence. The magnificent theatre, built in the first century A.D., holds up to 10,000 spectators, and the back of the stage still shows traces of the decorated colonnades. The frontage, over a hundred yards long and more than 40 yards high, is so impressive that Louis XIV proudly called it "the finest wall in my kingdom". Its grottoes are where the annual Foire d'Orange (page 109) takes place, and in the summer, from mid-July to the end of August, the grottoes house a permanent exhibition of Rhône wines.

The triumphal arch, built at about the same time as the theatre, is decorated with sumptuous sculpture representing trophies, battle scenes and floral designs. Apart from the main Roman remains, there are many other splendid relics of the period, all well preserved.

From Orange excursions can be planned so that most of the delightful villages and vineyards nearby can be visited. It is essential to follow the route on a detailed map, such as Michelin No. 81. Leave Orange on RN575 and procede to Camaret. From here, it may be worth making a short detour to the village of

Sérignan, where the great entomologist J.H. Fabre (1823–1915) lived for the last forty years of his life. The 'Harmas J.H. Fabre' is now a museum, and visitors can see his study and garden as well as many collections in the various rooms. Sérignan has a small woollen industry and, as elsewhere, olive oil and tomatoes are extensively cultivated. The wine of Sérignan is 85 per cent red and 15 per cent rosé, made from the Grenache, Carignan and Clairette grapes.

The route goes back part of the way and then turns off to Travaillan. The vineyards are planted on the vast stony plain, known as the '*Plan de Dieu*', where excellent red and rosé wines are made. They are of high alcoholic strength, yet supple in style, and are made mainly from the Grenache, Cinsaut and Mourvèdre.

Cairanne

A route—there are several in fact—through the vineyards leads to Cairanne, a neat little village on a small hill in an enormous green belt of vines. A conveniently-sited tourist office occupies its highest point, and a new church in modern architectural style overlooks the vineyards. There are ruins of a Gallo-Roman town here which archeologists have tried to associate with the mysterious 'Aeria', mentioned by the Greek Strabo in his geographical works written almost two thousand years ago. The tower, which belonged to the Knights Templar before they were dispersed and dispossessed in the fourteenth century, provides a fine view of the Rhône Valley, the majestic Ventoux range, the vast plain of Vaucluse and the Châteauneuf hills. This is one of the great viewpoints of the district. The tower also includes a museum that has a wine section, a gallery for works by local artists and free wine-tasting, so that it is a pleasant place in which to linger. There is interest for the antiquarian also, at the Neolithic cemetery.

From Cairanne it is a short drive to St. Cécile-les-Vignes, which has seen many civilisations in its 2,000 years. It is well known for its flower garden where the Rhône wine makers honoured Baron le Roy* with a statue, which was unveiled by the Baron himself. The town is of considerable interest with its old houses and quaint narrow streets. Due west are the vineyards of Rochegude, where the local pottery is well known.

Suze-la-Rousse

A few kilometres to the north is Suze-le-Rousse, a picturesque village with an imposing fourteenth century château which is now being converted into the Université du Vin and a museum. When the building is completed it will serve as the most important wine centre in the Rhône Valley. At the present time Rhône students have a choice of studying either at Beaune in Burgundy or at Montpellier, where there are excellent courses for viticulture and oenology. But still more space is needed for them.

This is one of the few châteaux which was spared by Richelieu, who destroyed all of the châteaux in the district in the seventeenth century. The base of the Château is twelfth century, with a Renaissance section added, and it was finally completed in the seventeenth century. In the large surrounding gardens there is a rather dilapidated Jeu de Paume (a real or royal tennis court) dating from the sixteenth century. This may, in due course, be renovated.

The modern laboratory which is being set up is ideal not only for advising growers but also for ensuring the strictest quality controls. Several rooms have already been rearranged into lecture theatres, and the original chapel has been converted into one of the most modern tasting rooms. Tasters sit in their individual booths with full facilities for tasting in perfect

* The late Baron le Roy de Boiseaumarie was one of the greatest authorities on Châteauneuf-du-Pape, and it was principally because of his efforts that this commune has attained its present high reputation. He followed this achievement by similar work with the Côtes-du-Rhônes *appellations*. Shot down as a pilot and severely wounded in World War I, it was not long after cessation of hostilities that he set about formulating a code of viticulture ensuring that quality, not quantity, was sought after by the growers. In 1923 the acceptance of control in this area preceded the national *Appellation Contrôlee* by twelve years.

conditions of light and temperature in a quiet and pure atmosphere.

Even while the installation is being established, courses are being arranged for growers not only to advise them and to teach them new methods of viticulture but also to encourage general tastings and discussion of legal, fiscal and labour problems. These courses normally last three to seven days. Other courses are planned for restaurateurs, sommeliers, merchants and distributors, in fact the general aim is to disseminate as much knowledge to as many people as possible, in the most idyllic atmosphere. During the summer, it is hoped that courses for amateurs will be held to place wine in its cultural context, not only considering wines themselves but also the history of wine and the development of legislation, with emphasis on tastings.

Bouchet is a small village of only 500 people which was founded in the twelfth century, and both the local church and the Cistercian Abbey date from this time. The high vaulted Abbey is now used as a cellar for fine wines in hogsheads (wooden casks, each holding about 215 litres) in tiers four high. The banqueting hall is used for local celebrations.

Tulette is a useful place to visit if you are on a camping holiday, as the local swimming pool and camping site are to be recommended! Slightly north-east (15 kilometres) of St. Maurice is Nyons, a charming quiet fourteenth century town, the meeting point of the regions of Tricastin and Rhône. It is famous for its olive oil, truffle markets and jam and fruit paste manufacture; its delightful climate with mild winters is ideal for exotic plants.

Both Villedieu and Buisson are towns also worth a visit, as they were founded in the twelfth century by the Templars. Then, by way of Visan, take the RN 976 northwards to Valréas, which was founded nine centuries ago. The ancient houses and Romanesque churches are a delight. Valréas was part of the Papal enclave within France until the late eighteenth century and is, together with Visan and two other villages, officially in the Vaucluse—although geographically it is in the Drôme département. A local monument stands to the memory of 53 hostages murdered by the Germans in 1944. The area is well known for its carton factories, which are used for packaging local produce such as fruits, vegetables, truffles and lavender.

From here, take the D46 to Vinsobres and then, via Mirabel-aux-Baronnies, follow the D538 down to Vaison la Romaine.

Vaison-la-Romaine

Its vineyards may be negligible today, but the excavated remains of the Roman city, dating from B.C. and sometimes described as a French Pompeii, are well worth seeing. The arena, the houses, the museum and the finely preserved bridge are all 'musts' for visitors to the area.

The medieval town is crowned by a twelfth century castle perched on a steep hill on the left bank of the Ouvèze. The Gallo-Roman town is on level ground opposite. The medieval Christian monuments are also noteworthy, in particular the fine Cathedral of Notre Dame, the cloister and the superb chapel of Saint-Quentin with a triangular Romanesque apse which is extremely rare.

The route continues westwards to Roaix, which was founded by the Templars in the twelfth century. Nearby and worth seeing are the two lovely villages of Sablet, with its towers and ramparts, and Séguret, which shares a wine co-operative with Roaix. It is a picturesque medieval village, and its annual Festival of the Arts creates tremendous interest.

Southwards on the picturesque foothills of the mountains is Gigondas, a quiet, compact village proud of its wines and historic associations. Wine and vine are the sole occupations and the wine was praised by Pliny centuries ago. The Bishops of Orange developed the vineyard in the fourteenth century. The village dominates the vineyards, looking like a *bourgade* (stronghold) of the Middle Ages.

Continuing on the D7 one arrives at Vacqueyras, a village within ancient ramparts in the shadow of the magnificent Ventoux mountains. The Romans discovered the thermal sulphur sources in the nearby mountains and the praises of Vacqueyras were sung in the twelfth century by one of the troubadours. From here it is worth making a small detour to visit Beaumes.

Beaumes-de-Venise and Carpentras

The vineyards of Beaumes-de-Venise, a delightful village with churches dating back to the eighth century, nestle on the foothills of the Ventoux range. Comparatively recent excavations unearthed many relics of the Gallo-Roman epoch including stone sarcophagi, funeral urns and stone weapons. Beaumes also saw the retreat of the Saracens when they were driven out of Provence in the eighth century. Cardinal Mazarin visited Beaumes in 1636 and the name of a stream in the neighbourhood commemorates his visit. The village is also mentioned in the works of Frédéric Mistral, the nineteenth century poet who revived the use of Provençal in the literary movement known as the Félibrige. Strange that the man who sang the praises of this fair province should have the same name as the relentless wind which so affects this area!

Continuing on the D7 takes us to Carpentras which, although not a wine producing town, is certainly worth stopping at. The well-preserved Gallo-Roman triumphal arch is the only part that remains of the fortified city walls put up by Pope Innocent VI in the fourteenth century. The cathedral, begun early in the fifteenth century by the Anti-Pope Benedict XII, the former episcopal palace (seventeenth century), the town hall and the synagogue (both eighteenth century) all deserve a visit.

From Carpentras, the D942 leads directly to the last stop on the Rhône Route—Avignon.

Avignon

The City of the Popes, Avignon is one of the great cities of France. It is almost entirely surrounded by fortifications, dating from the time when the Papal Court resided in the Palais des Papes, which is a mixture of residence and fortress. It is a magnificent example of medieval, civil and military architecture, built in the fourteenth century for Anti-Popes Benedict XII and Clement VI.

The Palais des Papes at Avignon

There are many churches dating back to the twelfth, fourteenth and sixteenth centuries, and several handsome medieval buildings—the Hôtel de Sade and Palais du Roure among them—mansions that were lived in by cardinals and many neoclassical houses. However, the city is probably most famous for its bridge, the Pont d'Avignon, popularised in the French song. Unfortunately it is now called the Bridge of St. Bénézet and is not much more than a long jetty over the river, with a small Romanesque and Gothic chapel on it which is dedicated to the saint of its name.

Other Local Drinks

Various delicious spirits and liqueurs are produced in the Rhône Valley, mainly for local consumption. As they are rarely exported, visitors should try at least some of them.

Eau de Vie de Marc is the brandy that is distilled from the fermented pulpy residues after the grapes have been pressed.

Distillation is usually undertaken in the village square in a mobile still, the kind that is moved around to do this particular work. Many years maturing in wood are essential to smooth the fiery flavour of this full-bodied spirit.

Fine is the brandy that is distilled from honest sound wine only. The brandy is checked by a tasting commission of the I.N.A.O. and is allowed the name of the wine's original *appellation*, plus the words *'Appellation'* and *'Réglementée'*. Light wines produce light brandy, fuller wines produce heavier brandies, but the final product is always of higher quality and greater elegance than the somewhat oily *marcs*.

Eaux-de-Vie are fruit brandies, strong, dry (because they have no additional sweetening) and colourless. Poire Williams *eaux-de-vie* are particulary excellent, being produced by the distillation of the fermented juice of the William pear. They have an exquisite fruity bouquet.

Apart from these spirits, several sweet liqueurs are also produced in the Rhône Valley.

Aiguebelle is a herb liqueur made by the monks of a Trappist abbey set in remote hills about ten miles from Montélimar. The liqueur is produced in two versions: green (the stronger) and yellow, and it is made by macerating several dozen Provençal plants, roots and herbs in alcohol. This is followed by slow distillation, maturation and sweetening. Aiguebelle has a spicy sweet flavour and possesses supposedly restorative properties.

Liqueur Poire William is sweetened *eau-de-vie de Poire William*, the pear spirit. It is made by the firm of Manguin in Avignon.

Grignan is a bitter-sweet herb liqueur made by monks in the Mont Ventoux region.

Myrtilles De Mont Pilat is a bilberry liqueur, produced from the myrtle shrub at St. Pierre de Boeuf near Condrieu. It is attractively packaged and is sweet, with a slightly herby tang.

La Sénancole is a yellow herb liqueur, aromatic and spicy, made by the monks of the Abbey de Sénanque. This Abbey was founded by the Cistercians in 1148 at Salon, Provence and according to local tradition Saint Bernard himself chose the site of the monastery.

It is recorded that one of the priors, Dom Marie Augustin, used local plants, which grew in abundance, to invent a delicately flavoured digestive which he named "La Sénancole" after the river that flows at the foot of the valley below the Abbey. The liqueur is now made in Cavaillon and the original Abbey is used as a museum and centre for social research.

Crème de Myrtilles is a new low strength bilberry liqueur (15 per cent alcohol) designed for mixing with Rhône rosé wines to make a refreshing sweetish apéritif. It is similar in style to '*un Kir*', the popular Burgundy apéritif made by mixing cassis—a blackcurrant liqueur—with dry white wine.

6

*Regional Gastronomy**

The Côtes du Rhône, with Lyon at its head and Provence at its feet, could hardly fail to be an exciting region for the itinerant gourmet. The gastronomy of the Rhône Valley sets off the magnificence of its wines. Perhaps the most obvious and best-known specialities are actually of Provençal origin; for this is the land of the olive and its oil, also of garlic; but there are other herbs, subtle in perfume and gentle in flavour, such as thyme, rosemary, basil, bay, fennel and sage, to enhance the dishes of the region.

Lyon, in the north, is often termed the capital of French gastronomy and the culinary centre of France. Lyon is famous for its sausages of many types, also the well-known *quenelle*, a light, delicate concoction of fish or meat, in an unctuous sauce; the best known is probably the *quenelle de brochet* (pike). Michelin cites the *poulet demi-deuil* (chicken in half mourning), so called because slivers of black truffles are inserted in the bird's flesh, and also mentions trout (from the mountain streams), the *rosette* (a type of regional salami), game, poultry, river fish from the Forez region and from the Vivarais (described as the "country of chestnut, boletus and all kinds of mushrooms"), fruits from every part of the countryside, plus, in the Bas-Dauphiné, a variety of *gratins*—dishes of sliced potatoes cooked in milk or in stock, with cheese or a cheese sauce.

Provence which, strictly, begins at Orange and extends down to the Mediterranean coast, has made a distinctive contribution

*Special thanks to my wife Elaine for drafting this chapter—P.H.

to the art of cooking and its influence is widespread. The Provençal cuisine differs considerably from that of the other French regions and, although it naturally makes use of the local produce, so rich and abundant, it has developed in a particular style, due to its having been an inhabited and highly civilised region—appreciating skilled cooks—for a very long time. The civilisation of ancient Rome, manifest in the numerous antiquities, has contributed to the culinary traditions of Provence, as has modern Italy. Much is also owed to the Greeks of classical times, who voyaged throughout the Mediterranean and brought with them not only foods but methods of cooking. Some of the Provençal stews, for example, are directly related to certain Greek recipes.

Restaurant Traditions

It is therefore no surprise to find, on reference to the current *Guide Michelin*, that the Rhône Valley restaurants positively glitter with the coveted 'stars'—symbols of restaurants offering food that is good (one star), very good and worthy of a détour (two) and, as far as the proud three star establishments are concerned, considered as being one of the best tables in France. Of twelve restaurants recently singled out for study in a book devoted to prestige restaurants, *Great Chefs of France* by Anthony Blake and Quentin Crewe (Mitchell Beazley, 1978), no less than six are within the Côtes du Rhône or its surrounding area.

These temples of '*haute cuisine*' are, of course exceptional as regards their tables and their cellars, but it is perhaps right to mention the Restaurant de la Pyramide at Vienne, even if all others must be left to those who can peruse the *Guide Michelin*—and can afford to visit such gastronomic stopping-places. For it was at the Pyramide that many who, today, are regarded as being in the top rank of the '*maîtres cuisiniers de France*' first stirred a sauce, under the critical eye of Fernand Point. Incomparable as a restaurateur, he was nevertheless proud of the fact that his staff called him 'Chef', as a practical tribute to his skill in the kitchen, rather than the more usual 'Patron' or 'Boss'. Point died in 1956, but his widow, together with many of his staff, maintain the standard of excellence set by her husband; indeed, he always admitted his debt to her as regards her ability to taste and buy wine. The cellars chez Point are remarkable. The wine list of the Pyramide in fact consists of several huge folders, each devoted to a single wine stocked by the house; there are several hundred 'local' wines, including the white Condrieu, used as the house open wine. It is probable that many of the thousands of customers who have dined at the Pyramide made their first acquaintance with fine Rhône wines by dining at this superb restaurant. Fernand Point's disciples have continued his tradition of excellence and have spread his gastronomic gospel to many other famous restaurants throughout France, so his influence is still great. A meal at the Pyramide is an unforgettable experience—although a costly one. However, even if you cannot treat yourself to a meal at any of the starred restaurants—and there are plenty of single stars that offer more modest prices on their set menus—there are also a huge number of more down to earth eating places where you can find delicious and interesting dishes.

À la Provençal

As soon as the middle of the Rhône region is reached, many dishes will bear the description '*à la Provençal*', which usually means that garlic and tomatoes are among the basic ingredients. But those who have memories of garlic as a very strong flavouring should not be deterred: the garlic of Provence is usually young and possesses a more delicate flavour than that of garlic bought in the U.K. For example, a *poulet aux quarante gousses d'ail* (chicken with forty cloves of garlic) is not as strong as might be supposed, but instead has a lightly impregnated savouriness. The most famous sauce of Provence, *aïoli*, is a garlic mayonnaise, and *aïgo bouïdo* (both terms are Provençal, not French) is a garlic soup. The locals' reverence for this marvellous vegetable is demonstrated by the reference to garlic soup being a '*sauvo la vida*'—a lifesaver. In fact, it is not only in Provence that garlic is considered beneficial to health and is associated with long life. Other specialities are *aigo sau*, a sort of stew of potatoes, onions, mushrooms, artichoke hearts, olive oil, water and fish—plus, of course, garlic; also *raïto*, which is a sauce made with onions, tomatoes, herbs, pounded walnuts, red wine—and garlic. These are real 'peasant dishes' and if you try and convince a small restaurant that you really do want to try them, you may be lucky and have a change from the rather bland food that Rhône restaurateurs think the British tourist prefers.

The tomatoes of the region are large and irregularly shaped, with a luscious flesh that possesses far more taste than the glasshouse tomatoes which are standard in the U.K. Provençal tomatoes both colour and flavour the many dishes in which they are used, and of course they are a delight in salads. Although mushrooms are commercially grown in Rousillon, south of Vienne, it is the wide variety of wild mushrooms to be found in woods and fields that should not be missed; I have a lasting memory of a luncheon with wine growers of Châteauneuf, at which a stupendous omelette was served, bursting with freshly-gathered *cèpes*—big, succulent mushrooms that make a feast of the most simple fare.

The herbs of Provence are justly famous. Not only do they enhance the cooking—they literally perfume the air, so that one drives through the countryside sniffing greedily! Juniper scents the undergrowth with its aroma and, on the wafting breezes, there are the pungent fragrances of fennel, rosemary, thyme, basil and savory. All find their way into the cooking pots and some are used in a herby Provençal cheese, *pebre d'aï. Fassum*, a dish of cabbage stuffed with herbs, is another local speciality—possibly of Middle Eastern or Greek origin.

Truffles (*truffes*) are to be found in Carpentras and Tricastin; in the latter place an *omelette aux truffes* is a great speciality. What sounds like another luxury dish is *asperges vauclusiennes*, but in fact this is a local culinary joke, for the 'asparagus' is a dish of globe artichokes, prepared *à la barigoule*—with ham and an array of herbs (thyme, rosemary, sage, juniper, laurel or bay, and wild thyme), plus onion and pimento.

Perhaps the most distinctive of all Provençal produce is the olive, which was introduced here by the Greeks at least 2,000 years ago. Olives feature in many dishes, as well as being served with drinks and in salads. They are used in cooking and, somewhat unusually to us Britons, in making pastry. A truly 'olivey' dish is *tapenade*, which is eaten as an appetizer; the Provençal for capers is *tapeno*, and capers are part of the recipe, plus pounded black olives, anchovies, tuna, lemon juice and olive oil.

Provençal cooking has received a new ingredient in recent times—rice, which is cultivated in the nearby Camargue. This is beginning to influence many dishes.

Fish and Meat

The tributaries of the Rhône, from both the east and the west, provide an abundance of fish, served in a variety of ways. These freshwater fish include crayfish (*écrevisse*), pike (*brochet*), perch (*perche*), carp (*carpe*), and also trout (*truite*), and they turn up on menus in one way or another: poached with various sauces, *au gratin* (with a cheese sauce) or, frequently, in the form of *quenelles*. These *quenelles* can be superb, seemingly simple but in fact very difficult to make; they are a type of light, delicate fish mousse, presented in a sausage or ball shape, poached and served with a complementary sauce. They are very much the '*gage d'or*' or party piece of a restaurant whose chef is demonstrating his or her skill, but the fortunate French housewife is now often able to buy them at the local *charcuterie* (as may the self-catering tourist or the more ambitious camper or caravanner). Another local speciality is *brandade de morue*, which is dried salt cod, reduced to a paste, with the addition of the ubiquitous olive oil and garlic. This recipe must surely have come from northern countries, whose traders packed the dried fish before setting sail. At its best, it can be light and delicious, somewhat like good *taramasalata*. Rather more esoteric, but of interest to any northern gourmet, is *cartigau d'anguilles*, which is an eel stew, or *limaces à la sucarelle*—snails cooked in white wine. Both these dishes are prepared with the usual Provençal accompaniments of olive oil, garlic and tomatoes.

Although a wide range of meat, game and poultry is found in the Rhône, the meat can be tough, due to the region's poor pastures; if it is, then it will be marinaded in wine with herbs, then cooked very gently with wine, onions and garlic. Each region here has its own particular *daube*, varied according to the local flavourings. Charollais beef is to be found in the north of the region, because this type of cattle is a speciality of Burgundy, and lamb also appears on many menus—the most delicious is probably that from the salty seaside pastures (*pré salé*) of the Camargue. Each town and, even, each village will have its own method of preparing the meat, as witness: *noisettes d'agneau brochette mistral* (noisettes of lamb on a skewer), *carré d'agneau aux herbes de Provence* (loin of lamb cooked with local herbs), *gigot d'agneau Avignonnaise*, or *à la Châteauneuvoise*, or *à la Drôme* (leg of lamb done in the style of Avignon, or Châteauneuf, or the Drôme) or *en croûte* (in a pastry case).

The famous *poulets de Bresse* (Bresse chickens, which in fact are so special that they have an *appellation contrôlée*) feature on menus in the north of the area. They are served in various local ways. Small birds are also popular—especially in Lirac—and spit-roasted thrushes (*grives*) are typical; birds that have fed on the local grapes are rightly relished!

As in many mountain regions, the cured ham of Mont Ventoux is a speciality. Game, such as hare (*lièvre*), rabbit (*lapin*) and boar (*sanglier*) will also be seen on menus, in addition to the various game birds. One curious local recipe is *cayettes de sanglier*, which is wild boar's liver mixed with bacon, boar's meat, herbs and wine, all stuffed into a sort of sausage skin and very much resembling a haggis, Provençal style!

Fruit and Cheese

Generally speaking, the cheeses of the Côtes-du-Rhône are made from goat's or sheep's milk, although one cow cheese of note is *Rigotte de Condrieu*. Some of the more interesting cheeses are *cachat* or *tomme du Mont Ventoux*—a strong flavoured cheese; *fromage de banon*—a small, flat cheese wrapped in chestnut or vine leaves; *bosson macérés*, made with olive oil, herbs, wine or *marc*, and the previously-mentioned *pebre d'aï* (or *poivre d'ane* as it is also known). From the Drôme there is a soft cheese made from goat's milk called *picodon*.

Many luscious fruits grow throughout the area. Figs (*figues*), quite different when fresh from the dried or tinned type and varying greatly between variety and variety, are rich and succulent. Pomegranates (*grenades*), peaches (*pêches*), apricots (*abricots*), melons (*melons*—but differently named according to type) and of course grapes (*raisins*) abound. The Cavaillon melons are perhaps the best known, as they are often exported to the U.K. Their scent heralds the sight of roadside stalls, groaning beneath the weight of mountains of melons. A delicious local way of serving melon is to scoop out the fruit, dust it with icing sugar and cover with local wine—refrigerated and served in wine glasses it makes a delectable conclusion to a meal. *Pastèque* is Provençal for the water melon which, when its seeds are scooped out and the hollow filled with Tavel or Châteauneuf du Pape and chilled, is equally enjoyable.

Sweetmeats

Fruits are not merely grown for the fresh fruit market but are much used in both confectionary and jam-making. Apt is a centre for crystallised fruits and for jams—especially for apricots preserved in this way.

One of the world's most famous sweets comes from Montélimar—in fact its name is synonymous with that of nougat. It was first made in the sixteenth century, when almond trees imported from Asia were planted in the Montélimar region;

it was found that, when the almonds were combined with the locally produced honey, a unique sweet resulted! Indeed, the scent of nougat perfumes the air around Montélimar as definitely as the herbs of Provence scent that region.

But Montélimar is by no means the only sweetmeat made in the region: almond crunch is widely manufactured, as are hard biscuits flavoured with almonds and honey. Many areas of France make *berlingots*, a hard sweet which Anglo-Saxons may interpret as 'satin cushions'; those of Carpentras are famous, with peppermint as the most popular of the flavourings.

Wine and Food

Inevitably, people ask which are the best wines to accompany certain foods, particularly when local specialities are being tried. The following is a general guide, suggestions made by the *Comité Interprofessional des Vins des Côtes du Rhône* in Avignon for the main and most widely distributed wines:

Côte Rôtie: small game (such as rabbit, hare and small birds), fillet of beef.
Crozes Hermitage: white—strongly flavoured sea fish; red—cheese and most meat.
Hermitage: white—fish and sea food in general, including crustacea and snails; red—roast meat and most game.
Tavel: white meats and poultry.
Châteauneuf-du-Pape: red—rich dishes, such as venison, wild boar, and fully flavoured ripe cheeses.
Côtes-du-Rhône and **Côtes-du-Rhône Villages:** beef (including stews), charcuterie and most cheeses.
And do not forget to serve the Muscat wines with dessert fruit.

APPENDIX 1

Tasting Wines

The tasting of wines can be a tiring and difficult job if too many samples are examined. Steady inhalation of bouquet will slowly anaesthetize the sensitive nasal buds; tasting too many samples will desensitize the taste buds in the mouth and on the tongue, so that minimal defects are no longer detectable. Experience will show how many samples you can taste with reasonable results, although they will usually require further examination and confirmation after the palate has been cleansed and rested.

Samples should, if possible, be tasted in large glasses which allow the bouquet to be examined and possibly give a hint of the grape varieties used in making the wine. Bouquet is especially important as every good wine offers its value 'on the nose'.

As a buyer, what is it that I look out for in my search for suitable wines? Remembering that I am buying very large quantities, the first rule is never to be rushed into making immediate decisions which may be coloured by the hospitality I am receiving.

My first task is to examine the colour of the wines. If I am looking at white wines, the young wines should be light in colour; red wines should have a purple edge. As white wines age they become darker, eventually golden. Red wines lose their purple and become deep red with age, then eventually lighter in their old age. As they age the wine colour tends to become brown at the edge of the glass. An indication of alcoholic strength is given by swirling the wine in the glass then watching the 'church window' patterns form from the glycerine in the richer wines.

My second job is to 'nose' every sample to obtain a first opinion. My grandfather used to say "a wine without nose is a wine without quality", and on this basis my first selection is completed. However, the wines with nose may not all have the characteristic bouquets I require, so these would be rejected as would those wines with unclean bouquets. Problem wines have unpleasant or abnormal bouquets which may be caused by many factors: infection (from too hot and/or fast fermentation), lack of care in cask, or contact with too much air when the wine was maturing. The bouquet may smell of stalks and pips, or of mould in damp years, or even of wood from a badly prepared cask. Occasionally there may be a metallic flavour from vat taps, or even a cement tang from the vat itself. If possibly don't taste unclean wines, as they will affect the palate badly.

The 'clean' wines are then ready for tasting. The bouquet can give a taster many clues, but it is the combination of nose and palate that is essential for balanced judgement. Only small quantities are needed for tasting. These should be swirled around the mouth at the same time that air is drawn in, and of course you should avoid swallowing! This aerated agitation gives all of your taste buds time to pass their messages to your brain to record an impression. Every last drop should be spat out and the 'after-taste' considered with great care, for the length of time the flavour lingers is very important, particularly when you are buying wines for a long time ahead. The taster must summarise the balance of the main factors of the wine—cleanliness with alcohol/acidity/sweetness for white wines and alcohol/acidity/tannin for red wines. Only experience can provide the ability to judge the characteristics of a few millilitres of wine, and great care needs to be taken—especially with young wines where the fruity flavour can mask a fault or imbalance.

The next sample of wine should not be taken until you have relaxed. In my opinion, if the taster wishes to eat between samples he should limit himself to white bread rolls. Never even consider nibbling cheese.

How many samples should you taste? This is a decision

which can only be made from practical experience, but certainly you will be able to tackle more when you are fresh in the morning than in late afternoon when you are tired. When you feel tired—stop. That is the time when your judgement will surely fail you and you may make a decision you will regret later.

The only important rule is that a clean glass should be used. Nothing else matters, although enjoyment can be immensely enhanced by serving wines in very thin or finely cut glasses. The excitement for the taste buds seems to increase in direct ratio to the decreasing thickness of the glass!

The enjoyment of wine usually follows a pattern: first there is the shape of the decanter or bottle. This anticipates the wine itself, and visually prepares the recipient for what is to follow. Next, you notice the colour of the wine and the way it flows from the bottle. This may stimulate the taste buds, producing a mouth-watering effect. Then comes the nosing of the wine, with the bouquet stimulating the nasal buds. After this you sip the wine, savouring the flavour on the palate. Finally, you swallow the wine. Enjoy the impression it makes on the back of the mouth, then contemplate the after-taste left on your palate. This should be an intensely pleasurable climax to your appreciation of the wine.

Personal Tasting

Having said all that, how should *you* go about selecting your wines? The most important factors are that you enjoy the flavour and can afford the wine. Never feel that you have to enjoy wine solely because it comes from a famous region or vineyard. Your decision should be based on the real qualities which your eyes and taste buds can enjoy—never persuade yourself that you ought to enjoy a particular wine because you have been told it's good. *You* must be the sole judge.

Give all your faculties plenty of opportunity to function with maximum benefit. Approach the tasting with a clean palate, and if necessary rinse your mouth to remove any lingering flavours of your last meal or hot drink. Make certain that your nose is clear and that you can breathe freely to really interpret the bouquet. Enjoy the bouquet and compare it with fruit or vegetable flavours—you will find that your brain charts the flavours to give you a 'grape variety' reaction, or even an 'unclean' reaction if all is not well with the wine. Assuming that you find the bouquet acceptable, taste the wine by swirling a small quantity around your mouth, avoiding swallowing, and then spit out as much as possible. By now you will have determined whether the wine is balanced, whether it has too much acidity, if the sweetness/dryness (of a white wine) suits your palate, and if the vital tannin in a red wine is acceptable as part of the wine or if it feels astringent and therefore makes the wine unbalanced and unpleasant for you. After you have ejected the sample, the lingering flavour must be pleasant—any unpleasant reaction at this stage signals possible trouble later.

In the early stages of your tasting career, you should try to find a selection of wines that you enjoy and some that you find less acceptable. Practise your tasting regularly and try to describe the wines to yourself so that you can differentiate between those you like and those you dislike. Use simple language and, more importantly, register fairly instant reactions.

Never be rushed into a decision and always take your time in selecting. A rushed decision may well be an expensive one and as much care as possible should be taken in deciding your purchases.

One final important point is that when you have made your decision, purchased your wine and taken it home, make certain that it is stored in a room with a cool temperature (55°F/13°C) so that the wine keeps well and matures slowly. There is nothing as disappointing as good wines which have been stored in too warm a place, therefore maturing much too fast and never realising their full potential.

APPENDIX 2

The Wine Orders of the Rhône Valley

Cornas

'Les Chevaliers de la Syrah et Roussette' is an order that was created in 1955. It promotes the fine wines from the noble grapes Syrah and Roussette.

Châteauneuf-du-Pape

The 'Échansonnerie des Papes' was created in 1967. It revives certain ceremonies of the ancient Pontifical Court and is particularly concerned with the promotion and appreciation of the wines, countryside monuments and customs of Châteauneuf-du-Pape. Ceremonies are held in the refurbished banqueting rooms of the Castle.

Tavel

'La Commanderie de Tavel' was founded in 1968, and all members must hold the diploma of the *École Dégustation de Tavel.* A special ceremony is held in honour of the vintage on the last Saturday of September, and at the end of April/early May there is a Chapter to celebrate the feast of Saint-Vincent.

Suze-la-Rousse

The 'Commanderie des Costes du Rhône' was founded in 1973. The Order defends and respects the grand viticultural traditions of the Côtes-du-Rhône wines. It promotes their reputation and development by means of fêtes, reunions and publicity. The Anniversary Chapter is held on May 11th, a Harvest Chapter takes place in early November, and other Chapters in France and abroad are organised from time to time.

APPENDIX 3

Wine Fairs in the Côtes-du-Rhône

January:	*Orange*—weekend nearest the 15th. Professional tastings and concours in the Amphitheatre Grottoes. (This is the only event restricted to trade tasters.) *Ampuis*—Sunday and Monday nearest to the 22nd (Saint Vincent). Marché aux Vins, a wine fair open to all.
March/April:	*Vinsobres*—the weekend 15 days after Easter. Agricultural and wine fair.
April:	*Villeneuve-lès-Avignon*—Sunday preceding Saint Mark (25th). Fair for Côtes-du-Rhône wines from the Gard and the Festival of Saint Mark. *Châteauneuf-du-Pape*—April 25th. Festival of Saint Mark, patron Saint of the Village. *Tavel*—last Sunday of April. Festival of Saint Vincent, the patron Saint of all growers.
May:	*Roquemaure*—Ascension Day. Festival of the wines of Roquemaure.
July:	*Orange*—July 11th to August 31st. Permanent exhibition of Côtes-du-Rhône wines in the Grottoes of the Amphitheatre.
July/August:	*Vacqueyras*—date fixed annually. Festival of wines from the Côtes-du-Rhône Villages *appellation*.

September:	*St. Péray*—first weekend of September. Festival of Wines (Fête des Vins). *Gigondas*—approximately September 27th. Messe des Vendanges (ceremonial Mass).
October:	*Tain l'Hermitage*—early October. Festival of the Vintage. *Crozes Hermitage*—last weekend of October. Festival of wine, including competitions.
November:	*Vaison-la-Romaine*—first fortnight (date fixed annually). Tasting/competition of Côtes-du-Rhône Primeurs (new wines of the same year). *Chavanay*—last Sunday of November. Marché aux Vins: the fine wines on Sunday and ordinary wines on Monday.
December:	*Cornas*—first Sunday. Marché aux Vins, a wine fair open to all.

The Appellations of the Rhône Valley

Appellation	Original decree	Rendement† (hectolitres per hectare)	P.L.C. (see page 124)	Minimum Alcohol	Vine Varieties
Côtes-du-Rhône	19/11/37 A.C.	50	Annual percentage *rapé* decided annually	11%	**Principal varieties:** Grenache, Clairette, Syrah, Mourvèdre, Picpoul, Terret noir, Picardan, Cinsaut, Roussanne, Marsanne, Bourboulenc, Viognier, Carignan (30% max.) **Secondary varieties** (30% max.): Counoise, Muscardin, Vaccarèse, Pinot (Bourgogne), Mauzac, Pascal blanc, Ugni blanc, Calitor, Gamay, Camarèse

Appellation	Original decree	Rendement† (hectolitres per hectare)	P.L.C. (see page 124)	Minimum Alcohol	Vine Varieties
Côtes-du-Rhône Villages	2/11/66 A.C.	35 (after *rapé*)	Annual percentage *rapé* decided annually	12.5% red 12% rosé and white	**Red wines:** Grenache (65% max.), Syrah, Mourvèdre, Cuisant (25%), other Côtes-du-Rhône rouge varieties (10% max.) **Rosé wines:** Grenache noir (60% max.), Camarèse, Cinsaut (15%), Carignan (15% max.), other Côtes-du-Rhône varieties (10% max.) **White wines:** Clairette, Roussanne, Bourboulenc (80% min.), Grenache blanc (10% max.), other Côtes-du-Rhône varieties (10% max.)

Châteauneuf-du-Pape	2/11/66 A.C.	35	*Rapé* between 5% and 20% fixed for each harvest	12.5%	**Principal varieties:** Grenache, Syrah, Mourvèdre, Picpoul, Terret noir, Picardan, Cinsaut, Clairette, Roussanne, Bourboulenc, Counoise, Muscadin, Vaccarèse
Gigondas	6/1/71 A.C.†	35 (excluding *rapé*)	*Rapé* fixed between 3% and 20%	12.5%	**Red wines:** Grenache (65% max.), Syrah, Mourvèdre and Cinsaut (total 25% min.) **plus** other Rhône varieties except Carignan (10% max.) **Rosé wines:** Grenache (60% max.), Cinsaut (15% min.), *plus* other Rhône varieties except Carignan (25% max.)

Appellation	Original decree	Rendement† (hectolitres per hectare)	P.L.C. (see page 124)	Minimum Alcohol	Vine Varieties
Tavel	15/5/36 A.C.	42	20% (lees, *vin de presse* for declassification, at least 10% of total)	11%	Grenache, Clairette blanche and rosé, Picpoul, Calitor, Bourboulenc, Cinsaut (15% min.) Mourvèdre, Syrah, Carignan (10% max.)
Côte Rôtie	18/10/40 A.C.	35	15%	10%	Syrah (80% min.), Viognier (20% max.)
Condrieu	27/4/40 A.C.	30	10%	11%	Viognier
Château Grillet	8/12/36 A.C.	32	10%	11%	Viognier
Hermitage and Crozes Hermitage	4/3/37 A.C.	40	10%	10%	**Red wines:** Syrah, **plus** Marsanne, Roussanne (15% max.) **White wines:** Marsanne, Roussanne

St. Joseph	15/6/56 A.C.	40	15%	10%	See Hermitage
Cornas	5/8/38 A.C.	35	15%	10.5%	Syrah
St. Péray	8/12/36 A.C.	40	15%	10%	Marsanne, Roussanne **Sparkling St. Péray:** Méthode Champenoise only
Clairette de Die	25/5/71 A.C.	50	20%	Clairette 9%, Muscat 9%; At marketing 10.5% for pure Clairette	Clairette, Muscat **Méthode dioise:** Muscat (50% min.); 4 months on lees during second fermentation in bottle. **Normal method:** If added as liqueur to first wine, then Clairette (75% min.); not less than 9 months on lees during second fermentation.

Appellation	Original decree	Rendement† (hectolitres per hectare)	P.L.C. (see page 124)	Minimum Alcohol	Vine Varieties
Côtes du Vivarais	8/8/62 V.D.Q.S.*	45		10.5%; with name of *Crû*, 11%	**Red & Rosé wines (principal varieties):** Cinsaut, Grenache, Mourvèdre, Picpoul, Syrah **Secondary varieties:** Autun, Carignan. **White wines:** Bourboulenc, Clairette, Grenache, Macabeu, Mauzec, Picpoul, Ugni blanc, Marsanne.
Lirac	14/10/47 A.C.	35	20%	11.5%	**White wines:** Clairette (33% min.), Bourboulenc, Ugni blanc, Maccabeo, Grenache, Picpoul, Calitor (25% each max.)

					Red & Rosé wines: Grenache (40% min.), Cinsaut, Mourvèdre (these three to be 60% min. of total), Clairette, Bourboulenc, Ugni blanc, Maccabeo, Syrah, Picpoul, Calitor, Carignan (10% max.)
Côteaux du Tricastin	27/7/73 A.C.‡	50	Decided annually	11%	**White wines:** Grenache blanc, Clairette, Picpoul blanc, Bourboulenc, **plus** Ugni blanc (30% max.) **Red & Rosé wines:** Grenache noir, Cinsaut, Mourvèdre, Syrah, Picpoul noir, **plus** Carignan (20% max.); Also 20% max. of white wine varieties.

Special Note:
If name of *Crû* is used (Orgnac, Saint-Montaut, Saint Remèze), then the following vine varieties are used for Red wines: Cinsaut, Grenache, Mourvèdre, Syrah, **plus** Carignan (25% max.), and for White wines: Bourboulenc, Clairette, Grenache, Marsanne, Picpoul.

Appellation	Original decree	Rendement† (hectolitres per hectare)	P.L.C. (see page 124)	Minimum Alcohol	Vine Varieties
Côtes du Lubéron	20/12/51 V.D.Q.S.*	45	Decided annually	10.5%	**White wines (principal varieties):** Clairette, Bourboulenc **Secondary varieties:** Grenache blanc, Pascal blanc, Roussanne, Ugni blanc. **Red & Rosé wines (principal varieties):** Grenache, Syrah, Mourvèdre, Cinsaut, Counoise, **plus** Carignan (50% max.) **Secondary varieties** (30% max.): Pinot Bourgogne, Gamay, Picpoul **plus** varieties permitted for white wines.

Côtes du Ventoux	27/7/73 A.C.	50	20%	11%	**White wines (principal varieties):** Clairette, Bourboulenc **Secondary varieties** (30% max.): Grenache blanc, Roussanne, Ugni blanc, Picpoul blanc, Pascal blanc **Red & Rosé wines (principal varieties):** Grenache noir, Syrah, Cinsaut, Mourvèdre, Carignan (30% max.) **Secondary varieties** (20% max.): Picpoul noir, Counoise, Clairette, Bourboulenc, Grenache blanc, Roussanne, Ugni blanc, Picpoul blanc, Pascal blanc

*All wines require analysis and tasting for the V.D.Q.S. label.

† Annual Committee of 4 growers and 2 merchants nominated by the I.N.A.O. to fix the *rapé* percentage and any change in basic *rendement*.

‡ All wines certified by an I.N.A.O. panel before sale.

THE RHÔNE VINTAGES 1965–1978

Quantity in hectolitres (1 hectolitre = approx. 22 gallons)

	1978	1977	1976	1975	1974	1973	1972
Côte Rôtie	3,077	2,108	2,132	1,468	1,831	2,927	1,428
Condrieu	96	115	176	105	122	206	66
Château Grillet	29	63	87	40	87	84	28
St. Joseph	5,726	3,812	4,684	2,188	4,310	4,093	1,962
Crozes Hermitage	27,106	17,548	20,014	17,748	21,044	27,997	19,768
Hermitage	3,136	3,159	3,304	2,022	3,859	4,108	3,356
Cornas	1,551	1,354	1,424	810	1,586	2,029	1,145
St. Péray	1,061	1,646	1,447	880	1,716	1,447	1,183
Châteauneuf-du-Pape	90,398	86,466	93,333	62,660	80,499	98,472	71,398
Gigondas	31,416	23,166	27,729	17,503	26,753	30,601	26,634
Tavel	30,624	29,161	28,426	19,971	28,722	28,055	21,841
Lirac	16,175	10,741	10,077	10,704	11,724	24,404	13,870
Côtes du Rhône Villages*	109,263	65,241	68,728	79,396	70,277	154,506	69,283
Côtes du Rhône	1,538,346	1,358,189	1,514,862	991,638	1,260,761	1,363,784	1,154,487
Total	**1,858,004**	**1,601,280**	**1,776,423**	**1,207,131**	**1,513,291**	**1,742,713**	**1,386,449**
Beaumes de Venise	6,922	4,604	5,185	3,294	5,113	5,172	3,403
Rasteau	3,099	1,087	2,363	1,722	2,335	2,803	2,723
Côtes du Ventoux	195,121	129,762	166,227	109,140	124,499	163,201	116,106
Côteaux du Tricastin	69,189	49,840	48,394	—	—	—	—
Côtes du Vivarais	31,876	17,038	14,922	—	—	—	—

**C.D.R. Sup. Growth plus C.D.R. Villages*

1971	1970	1969	1968	1967	1966	1965
669	2,379	787	1,135	1,443	2,504	1,301
129	140	19	173	81	141	159
66	66	26	67	42	24	25
1,661	3,177	1,310	1,492	2,371	2,321	1,729
13,203	19,739	10,964	7,802	12,755	11,701	9,757
3,128	5,632	2,524	2,063	4,091	4,818	4,344
1,022	1,805	874	773	1,280	1,276	1,279
1,458	1,468	748	1,025	1,260	1,263	1,839
92,272	92,627	62,461	53,563	86,986	76,075	83,435
—	—	—	—	—	—	—
26,983	24,984	14,753	14,943	21,687	16,853	18,490
6,786	4,792	4,615	4,756	6,112	5,734	5,434
142,346	152,539	61,373	63,510	83,367	—	—
1,047,947	1,179,006	678,348	625,339	943,428	1,002,726	946,520
1,348,190	**1,478,370**	**838,802**	**776,641**	**1,176,439**	**1,125,436**	**1,074,312**
4,441	4,448	—	—	—	—	—
3,056	3,756	—	—	—	—	—
135,566	—	—	—	—	—	—
—	—	—	—	—	—	—
—	—	—	—	—	—	—

Glossary

Appellation d'Origine Contrôlée	The quantity control for quality wines which also defines permitted vine varieties, maximum yield per hectare and other criteria (see pages 60 to 63).
le Bigot	The special hoe used on the steep slopes of the Northern Rhône.
Cave	The cellar.
le Caviste	Cellar worker.
le Cep	The vine, vinestock.
le Cépage	The specific vine variety.
le Climat	A named part of a vineyard.
Collage	Fining—the process of clarification prior to bottling.
Corps	Body—refers to the fullness of a wine.
Côte	Slope (*Côtes* is a term used in the Rhône to define a whole area).
un Coteau	A hillside or little slope.
un Crû	A specific growth.
la Cuve	The vat.

une Cuvée	A specific wine from a particular vatting or estate. *Tête de cuvée*—the grower's finest wine.
Dégustation	Tasting.
le Dépôt	Deposit in wine.
la Domaine	Vineyard(s) belonging to the same proprietor. A single estate may have a geographical, fancy or grower's name after it.
Dur	Hard—refers to harsh red wines.
Égrappage	The process of removing the stalks before fermentation.
Fin	Fine, as in a choice wine.
la Fleuraison	The flowering of the vine in spring or early summer.
le Foudre	A wooden cask of unspecified size.
la Foulage	The process of mashing or crushing the grapes.
le Fouleur	The machine which breaks up grapes before fermentation.
le Goût	Taste. *Goût de terroir*—of the soil; *goût de bois*—of wood.
Hectare	The metric land measure (1 Hectare = 2.47 acres).
I.N.A.O.	*l'Institut National des Appellations d'Origine* is the National Governmental Organisation which controls growers and draws up the individual rules for each specific *appellation*.

le Lie — The lees formed as a deposit during fermentation or later when red wine matures in cask.

Madérisé — An oxidised wine (a derogatory term).

Méthode Champenoise — Sparkling wine made by the Champagne method.

Millésimé — The vintage date of the wine, marked with a vintage.

Mise à la Domaine — Estate bottled.

Mise au Château — Château bottled.

Mise en bouteille — Bottled by.

le Moût — The must—unfermented grape juice.

Mûr — Ripe (of grapes), mellow/mature (of wine).

Mutage — The addition of alcohol to wine or must.

un Négociant — A (wholesale) merchant.

Ouillage — Ullage—the topping up of casks which is necessary due to evaporation through the wood.

une Pièce — A wooden cask, 215/225 litres in capacity.

P.L.C. — *Plafond Limité de Classement*—the maximum amount by which the *rendement* may be exceeded before the whole crop is declassified to a lower (and less valuable) *appellation* (see page 61).

la Pourriture	Rot which affects the vines.
le Pressoir	The wine press.
le Primeur	The new wine of the most recent vintage.
une Propriétaire	An owner (of a property).
le Pupitre	The rack for holding bottles of sparkling wine upside-down during the second fermentation.
le Quartier	Part of a vineyard (literally, the quarter).
Rancio	Rancid.
la Récolte	The harvest or vintage.
la Remontage	The pumping of fermenting wine over the cap of skins, pips, stalks, etc., during fermentation to keep the solids below the liquid surface.
le Rendement	The maximum production, in hectolitres of wine per hectare of vineyard, permitted by the *Appellation Contrôlée* applying to the particular area.
Sec	Dry.
Soufre	Sulphur: SO_2 gas or any solution necessary to preserve wine.
le Soutirage	The racking of wine from one cask to another to separate wine from lees; can be arranged in presence or absence of air.
le Tonnelier	The cooper.

le Triage — The separation of unripe or damaged grapes from the main crop.

V.D.N. — *Vin doux Natural* (see page 56).

V.D.Q.S. — *Vin Délimité de Qualité Supérieure*—quality wine with strict qualifications, including tasting, for permission to use the 'label'. *V.D.Q.S.* is a lower grade than *Appellation Contrôlée.*

le Vendange — The harvest, vintage.

le Vigneron — Grower.

Vin de garde — A wine for laying down.

Vin mousseux — Sparkling wine.

Some Wine Cellar Addresses

Ampuis 69420: E. Guigal, Route Nationale, Tél: (74)* 85.40.11.

Aubignan 84190: Domaine de Saint-Sauveur, route de Caromb, Tél: (90) 65.01.34

Bagnols-sur-Cèze 30200: Arène et Fils, Le Haut-Castel, Route de Barjac, Tél: (66) 89.67.19.
Jean-Claude Chinieu, Domaine de Lindas, Route de Pont-Saint-Esprit, Tél: (66) 89.65.70.
Domaine de Signac, Route d'Orsan, Tél: (66) 89.58.47.

Beaumes de Venise 84190: Cave des Vignerons, Tél: (90) 65.00.48.

Bouchet 26130: Abbaye de Bouchet, Tél: (75) 04.83.21.

Cairanne 84290: A Brusset et Fils, Le Village et Caveau du Plan de Dieu, Tél: (90) 30.82.16.
Caveau du Belvedere, Tél: (90) 30.83.48.
Cave des Coteaux, Tél: (90) 30.82.05.
Rabasse Charavin, Coteaux St. Martin, Route de Rasteau, Tél: (90) 30.82.27.

* The dialling codes of the *départements* are given in brackets, and these should be used if you are telephoning from outside the area.

Châteauneuf-du-Pape 84230: (There are a large number of establishments here, in addition to those mentioned).
Les Fines Roches, Tél: (90) 39.70.30.
Charles Mestre, 17 rue Alphonse Daudet, Tél: (90) 39.72.27.
Domaine de Mont-Rédon, Tél: (90) 39.72.75.
Père Anselme, Tél: (90) 39.70.07.
Caveau des Reflets, Avenue Boise-de-la-Ville, Tél: (90) 39.71.07.
Domaine Trintignant, 11 route d'Avignon, Tél: (90) 39.70.95.

Chusclan 30200: Cave des Vignerons, Tél: (66) 89.63.03.

Condrieu 42410: Caveau de Viognier, 1 rue Nationale, Tél: (74) 59.52.22.

Cornas 07130: Auguste Clape, Tél: (75) 60.33.64.
Marcel Juge, Grande-Rue, Tél: (75) 60.36.68.
Robert Michel, Grande-Rue, Tél: (75) 60.38.70.
Alain Voge, Rue du Midi de de l'Enquerre, Tél: (75) 60.32.04.

Courthézon 84350: Cave Cooperative Vinicole—Le Cellier des Princes, R.N.7., Tél: (90) 70.70.24.

Gigondas 84190: Caveau du Gigondas, Place de la Mairie.
Cave des Vignerons, Tél: (90) 65.86.27.
Roger Meffre, Domaine St. Gayan, Tél: (90) 65.86.33.

Lirac 30290: Château de Ségriès, Tél: (66) 21.85.35.

Orange 84100: Arnaud Daumen, Quartier du Grès, Tél: (90) 34.20.10.
Michel Bernard, Route de Sérignan, Tél: (90) 34.35.17.
Réné Chastan et Fils, Domaine Palestor, Tél: (90) 34.07.41.
Roger Jaume et Fils, Domaine des Chanssaud, Cabrières, Tél: (90) 34.23.51.
Domaine Pierre Quiot, Domaine de Maucoil, Quartier du Grès, Tél: (90) 34.14.86.

Pont-Saint-Esprit 30130: Cave Cooperative, Avenue Vigan-Braquet, Tél: (66) 82.70.65.
Pierre Coste, Domaine de Laplagnol, Quartier Masconil, Tél: 82.72.50.
Remoulins 30210: Cave Cooperative Vinicole, Route d'Avignon, Tél: (66) 87.01.51.

Rasteau 84110: Cave des Vignerons, Tél: (90) 36.12.32.
Maurice Charavin, Domaine du Char à Vin, rue de la Poste, Tél: (90) 36.12.47.

Rochefort du Gard 30650: Les Vignerons du Castelas, Tél: (90) 31.72.10.

Roquemaure 30150: J.-C. Assemat, Domaine des Causses et Garrigues, Tél: (66) 89.23.52.
Cave Co-operative Agricole de Vinification des Vignerons, 1, rue des Vignerons, Tél: (66) 89.20.01.
Achille Granier, Domaine de la Croze, rue des Vétérans, Tél: (66) 89.41.73.
Marie Pons Mure, Domaine de Castel Oualou, Tél: (66) 89.20.64.
Antoine Verda, Château Saint-Roche, Tél: (66) 89.20.59.

Sablet 84110: Cave Co-operative 'Le Gravillas', Tél: (90) 36.90.20.
Louis Chamfort, Domaine de Verquière, Tél: (90) 36.90.11.

Sainte-Cécile-les-Vignes 84290: Max Aubert, Domaine de la Présidente, Route de Cairanne, Tél: (90) 30.80.34.
Caveau-Chantecotes, 7, cour du Portalet, Tél: (90) 30.83.25.
Abel Sahuc, Domaine de la Grande Ribe, route de Bollène, Tél: (90) 30.83.75.
Cave des Vignerons réunis, route de Valréas, Tél: (90) 30.80.28.

Saint-Gervais 30200: Cave des Vignerons, Tél: (66) 89.67.05.
Guy Steinmaier, Domaine Sainte-Anne, Caveau des Cellettes, Tél: (66) 89.67.41.

Saint-Laurent-des-Arbres 30126: Cave des Vins du Cru de Lirac, Tél: (66) 89.34.02.
Lombardo Frères, Domaine 'Le Deves', Tél: (66) 89.34.23.
Charles Pons Mure, Domaine de la Tour, Tél: (66) 89.34.19.

Saint-Maurice-sur-Eygues 26110: Cave Co-operative des Coteaux, Tél: (75) 3.

Saint-Pantaléon-les-Vignes 26230: Cave Co-operative, Tél: (75) 26.26.43.

Saint-Péray 07130: Caveau de Dégustation, 21, rue Ferdinand-Malet, Tél: (75) 60.31.63.

Seguret 84110: Les Vignerons de Roaix-Seguret, Tél: (90) 36.91.13.

Sérignan du Comtat 84100: Cave Co-operative et Caveau, les Coteaux du Rhône, Tél: (90) 70.00.04.

Sorgues 84700: A. Ogier, Chemin du Fournalet, Tél: (90) 39.18.31.

Suze-la-Rousse 26130: Château de l'Estagnol, M. Chambovet, route de Grignan, Tél: (75) 04.81.38.

Tain l'Hermitage 26600: Cave Co-operative de Vins Fins, Route de Larnage, Tél: (75) 08.20.87.
Chapoutier, avenue de la Republique, Tél (75) 08.28.65.
Paul Jaboulet Aîné, rue Monier No. 8/10, Tél: (75) 08.22.65.

Tavel 30126: Christian Amido, Tél: (66) 89.24.14.
Levêque, Cave du Seigneur de Vaucrose, Route de Lirac, Tél: (66) 89.23.37.
Domaine Maby, Tél: (66) 89.24.16.
Château de Manissy, Tél: (66) 50.04.16.
Les Vignerons de Tavel, Tél: (66) 89.24.57.

Tournon-sur-Rhône 07300: Jean-Louis Grippat, Quartier de 'La Sauva', Ancienne route de Mauves, Tél (75) 08.15.51.

Tulette 26130: Cave Costebelle, route d'Orange, Tél: (75) 04.86.02.

Vacqueyras 84190: Archimbaud, Le Clos de Cazaux et Château de Montmirail, Tél: (90) 65.84.62.
Caveau des Dentelles de Montmirail, Place de l'Eglise, Tél: (90) 65.86.62.
Cave des Vignerons, Tél: (90) 65.84.54.
Lambert Frères, Domaine des Lambertins, Tél: (90) 65.85.54.
Rémy Mayre, Domaine du Mousquetaire, Tél: (90) 65.84.96.

Vaison-la-Romaine 84110: Co-operative Vinicole de Vaison et du Haut-Comtat, Tél: (90) 36.00.43.

Valréas 84600: Romain Bouchard, Domaine du Vale-des-Rois, Tél: (90) 35.04.35.
Maison des Vins, 11, avenue Charles-de-Gaulle, Tél: (90) 35.06.80.
Syndicat des Vignerons, Caveau de Dégustation, Place de la Mairie, Tél: (90) 35.04.71.

Verin 42410: Neyret-Gachet, Château Grillet près Verin—by appointment made in advance only—Tél: (74) 59.51.56.

Villedieu 84110: Cave Co-operative 'La Vigneronne', Villedieu-Buisson, Tél: (90) 36.23.11.

Vinsobres 26110: Co-operative Vinicole Vinsobraise, Tél: 17
Cave du Prieurée, Tél: 26.
François Vallot, Domaine du Corançon, Tél: (75). 26.03.24.

Visan 84600: Cave Co-operative Les Coteaux, Tél: (90) 91.12.

Further reading

Although all reference books dealing with wine in general have a section devoted to the wines of the Rhône, it is—surprisingly enough—not easy to find any specific works on the subject in English. Therefore I have included some helpful French books which are easy to obtain; even a superficial knowledge of the language should be sufficient to enable travellers to gain useful information by referring to them.

The Wines of the Rhône—John Livingstone-Learmonth and Melvyn C.H. Master (Faber, 1978)

Great Chefs of France—Anthony Blake and Quentin Crewe (Mitchell Beazley, 1978)

In French:

Histoire de la Vigne et des Grands Vins des Côtes-du-Rhône—Robert Bailly (privately printed by the C.I.V.C.D.R., Maison du Vin, 41 Cours Jean Jaurès, Avignon)

Parcours du Vignoble (Itineraries and addresses of cellars) is also available from the Maison du Vin

The Michelin Green Guides: *Vallée du Rhône, Vivarais, Lyonnais*, and *Provence* are worth consulting, as is the Michelin Red Guide.

Index